S. HRG. 113–656

IRAQ AT A CROSSROADS: OPTIONS FOR U.S. POLICY

HEARING

BEFORE THE

COMMITTEE ON FOREIGN RELATIONS UNITED STATES SENATE

ONE HUNDRED THIRTEENTH CONGRESS

SECOND SESSION

JULY 24, 2014

Printed for the use of the Committee on Foreign Relations

Available via the World Wide Web: http://www.gpo.gov/fdsys/

U.S. GOVERNMENT PUBLISHING OFFICE

94–805 PDF   WASHINGTON : 2015

For sale by the Superintendent of Documents, U.S. Government Publishing Office
Internet: bookstore.gpo.gov   Phone: toll free (866) 512–1800; DC area (202) 512–1800
Fax: (202) 512–2104   Mail: Stop IDCC, Washington, DC 20402–0001

CONTENTS

IRAQ AT A CROSSROADS: OPTIONS FOR U.S. POLICY

THURSDAY, JULY 24, 2014

U.S. SENATE,
COMMITTEE ON FOREIGN RELATIONS,
Washington, DC.

The committee met, pursuant to notice, at 10:04 a.m., in room SD–419, Dirksen Senate Office Building, Hon. Robert Menendez (chairman of the committee) presiding.

Present: Senators Menendez, Boxer, Cardin, Shaheen, Coons, Durbin, Murphy, Kaine, Markey, Corker, Risch, Rubio, Johnson, Flake, McCain, and Barrasso.

OPENING STATEMENT OF HON. ROBERT MENENDEZ, U.S. SENATOR FROM NEW JERSEY

The CHAIRMAN. Good morning. This hearing will come to order. Today we focus on Iraq and U.S. policy options, but to fully examine the crisis in Iraq we must acknowledge the broader context of developments across the region. Earlier this year I held a hearing on the spillover from the Syria conflict to examine the implications of continued violence in Syria and how it would impact the stability and security of neighboring countries. Now we are seeing the very dangerous results of that spillover with the advancement of ISIS, the increase in sectarian violence, underscored by the dissolution of any real border between Iraq and Syria, and the designation by ISIS of a caliphate across Syria and Iraq that is threatening to create a security vacuum in the heart of the Middle East.

While today's hearing will not focus specifically on the regional threat posed by ISIS or on United States-Syria policy, I want to take this opportunity to restate my long-held position that we must enhance our support to the moderate Syrian opposition, the only ones willing to challenge ISIS and other al-Qaeda affiliates in Syria. It seems to me at the end of the day supporting these moderate forces must be one pillar of a broader U.S. policy in the region.

No one should be surprised that Iraq is the victim of this spillover, but we should be extremely concerned by the rapid expansion of ISIS and alarmed by Iran's clear involvement in Iraq. And we should be dismayed by the convenient alignment of Iranian, Russian, and Syrian interests in response to recent developments, especially in Iraq. At its core, this alignment is about self-preservation of rogue actors that seek to maintain power by destabilizing others and keeping weak governments susceptible to malign influence.

In my view, Iraq does not have to proceed down this path and it is up to Iraq's leaders to chart a different course for their country.

I am deeply disappointed that, after years of United States investment in time and resources, the loss of thousands of American lives, and the commitment of billions of dollars to support Iraq's political development and the creation of a responsible, capable Iraqi Security Force, that they deserted the communities they were responsible for protecting, abandoned United States military equipment, and fled from ISIS fighters.

At the same time, ISIS's expansion across Iraq and its reception by Iraq's Sunni communities and tribes would not have been possible except for the accumulation of years of destructive sectarian, corrupt policies by the central government in Baghdad. Iraq has the potential to be an economically prosperous, diverse, and politically representative model for others in the region, but Iraqi leaders have focused on their own sectarian and ethnic interests for too long, at the expense of building an Iraq for all Iraqis.

The time is now for Iraq's elected leaders to form a national unity government that is truly representative. I applaud the recent progress in nominating a Speaker and two Deputy Speakers for Iraq's Parliament and today's promising news that a President has been named. I encourage Iraq's leaders to continue this critical work and finalize the government with leaders committed to leading an Iraq for all Iraqis.

While Iraq's leaders continue negotiations to form the next government, the Department of Defense has completed the assessment of Iraqi Security Forces. I look forward to hearing from our administration witness on the findings and recommendations provided by U.S. advisers and plans going forward to counter the threat from ISIS and Congress' role in this effort.

Let me take a moment to highlight the particularly dangerous situation of minority communities in Iraq and particularly Iraqi Christians. I recently joined Senator Stabenow in a meeting with Archbishop Bashar Warda from the Chaldean Diocese of Erbil. His description of the terror that ISIS has inflicted in Iraqi Christian communities is truly horrifying, and I hope that our witnesses today will share with us steps the administration is taking to address the urgent and unique situation of Iraqi Christians.

I hope to hear from our administration witnesses today whether or not they believe Iraqi leaders are capable, or able, I should say, to form a more representative government, what is required to turn the tide against ISIS, and if there is a new national unity government in Baghdad what should we do to demonstrate support.

With that, Senator Corker.

OPENING STATEMENT OF HON. BOB CORKER, U.S. SENATOR FROM TENNESSEE

Senator CORKER. Thank you, Mr. Chairman. I want to thank our witnesses for being here.

Iraq seems to be disintegrating as the terrorist organization ISIS now controls Mosul, Iraq's second-largest city, Fallujah, and much of Ramadi, parts of Baiji, Tikrit. Though significantly outnumbered, ISIS managed to overwhelm entire divisions of the Iraqi

Army, many of whom removed their uniforms and ran. ISIS also has claimed credit for a recent string of bombings in Baghdad, is responsible for systemic persecution of Christians, thousands of whom are being forced to flee their homes under penalty of death if they do not convert and pay a tax.

The U.N. reports that last month was the deadliest in Iraq since 2008, with 2,400 Iraqis killed, two-thirds of which were civilians.

For those of us who were here during the debate over the hard-won gains of the surge, this is hardly an outcome that would have been imagined back then. Though our intelligence picture in Iraq is woefully inadequate, the situation should not surprise us, for two reasons. The crisis is connected to the disaster in Syria, which our country has largely ignored. Sunni militants have long enjoyed freedom of movement across the porous border in Anbar province and had been in control of Fallujah and key parts of Ramadi for months prior to the takeover of Mosul.

Since 2009, Maliki has systematically shredded and politicized the entire structure of the Iraqi Security Forces, replacing competent commanders with incompetent, yet loyal, commanders and creating a more sectarian institution that scares the average Iraqi as much as ISIS.

Despite the connection to Syria, it is important to note that this is not just an invasion from foreign fighters. ISIS simply cannot hold this much territory in Iraq while maintaining operations in Syria without help on the ground. Whether we can look—rather, we can look at this as a civil and sectarian war being exacerbated and exploited by a growing terrorist threat. This is yet another signal of how badly Prime Minister Maliki has alienated the Sunni population.

Even if Maliki leaves, without political reconciliation among Iraq's key communities no amount of military support can make a difference. But on the other hand, if we do not help the Iraqi Government survive and hold territory now, there is a possibility we will not be discussing political reconciliation in a few months because the country could break apart.

Today in this hearing I hope we can confront this dilemma head on. I hope we can start to identify the right mix of security assistance and political steps that will help get the country back on the right track. I am open to working with the administration to determine what we can do as a nation to help shore up the defenses of the Iraqis and encourage political reconciliation among Iraqi leaders.

I want to thank you for being here today. I look forward to this hearing and I look forward to us weighing in on what we believe are the most appropriate steps forward. Thank you very much.

The CHAIRMAN. Thank you, Senator Corker.

Let me introduce our first panel. With us today is Deputy Assistant Secretary of State for Iraq and Iran, Brett McGurk, who has just returned from a 6-week trip to Iraq, where he was assisting the Embassy team; and Ms. Elissa Slotkin, performing the duties of the Principal Deputy Under Secretary of Defense for Policy, whose experience on Iraq ranges from the intelligence community to the National Security Council to the State Department, and now to the Defense Department.

Let me remind both of you that your full statements will be included in the record without objection. I would ask you to summarize in about 5 minutes or so, so that the members of the committee can engage with you in a dialogue. With that, we will start with you, Mr. Secretary.

STATEMENT OF BRETT McGURK, DEPUTY ASSISTANT SECRETARY OF STATE FOR IRAQ AND IRAN, U.S. DEPARTMENT OF STATE, WASHINGTON, DC

Mr. McGurk. Thank you. Good morning. Chairman Menendez, Ranking Member Corker, members of this committee, I thank you for inviting us to discuss the situation in Iraq, with a focus on U.S. response since the Islamic State of Iraq and the Levant attacked Mosul nearly 7 weeks ago.

Let me first review the bidding on why this matters. ISIL is al-Qaeda. It may have changed its name, it may have broken with senior al-Qaeda leadership such as Ayman al-Zawahiri, but it is al-Qaeda in its doctrine, ambition, and increasingly in its threat to U.S. interests. Should there be any question about the intentions of this group, simply read what its leader, Abu Bakr al-Baghdadi, says. And it is important to pay attention to what he says because we cannot risk underestimating the goals, capacity, and reach of this organization.

Baghdadi in May 2011 eulogized the death of Osama bin Laden and promised a violent response. ISIL training camps in Syria are named after Osama bin Laden. In his audio statements Baghdadi regularly issues veiled threats against the United States, promising a direct confrontation. And, in his feud with al-Zawahiri. Baghdadi is clearly seeking to lead the global jihad.

Additionally, ISIL is no longer simply a terrorist organization. It is now a full-blown army, seeking to establish a self-governing state through the Tigris and Euphrates Valleys in what is now Syria and Iraq. It now controls much of eastern Syria. In January in Iraq it moved into Anbar province, taking control of Fallujah, and on June 10 it moved on Mosul.

I arrived in Erbil, 80 kilometers east of Mosul, on June 7 and I will begin there. In meetings with local officials from Mosul and with Kurdish officials on June 7, we received early indications that ISIL was moving in force from Syria into Iraq and staging forces in western Mosul. We immediately asked and received permission from Kurdish leaders to deploy Peshmerga forces on the eastern side of the city, but the Government of Baghdad did not share the same sense of urgency and refused the deployments.

Iraqi military commanders promised to send nine brigades of force to Mosul in response to our warnings. We stressed, however, that the forces might not arrive in time.

On June 9, the situation remained extremely tense and we continued to urge the immediate deployment of additional security forces to protect against an ISIL attack from west to east. In the early hours of June 10, ISIL launched a complex suicide bomb attack across a strategic bridge and poured forces into the eastern part of the city. Iraqi resistance totally collapsed, which led to a panic and a snowballing effect southward through the Tigris Valley and to the cities of Tikrit, Samarra, and Bilad.

The result was catastrophic. Five divisions nearly dissolved and the approaches to Baghdad were immediately under threat. I flew to Baghdad first thing that morning with a focus on ensuring our people were safe, working with Ambassador Beecroft and our team, and working with the Iraqis to ensure the northern approaches to Baghdad were bolstered.

My written testimony sets forth in detail the critical elements of our crisis response. We first made certain that our people would be safe, including contractors working on bases outside of Baghdad, who were evacuated with the help of the Iraqi Air Force. At the Embassy and at the airport, we rebalanced staff to manage the crisis and brought in additional Department of Defense resources to ensure the security of our facilities.

In parallel, at the President's direction, we worked to urgently improve our intelligence pictures throughout western and northcentral Iraq, surging surveillance flights, establishing joint operations centers, and deploying Special Operations Forces to assist Iraqi units around the capital. These intelligence and security initiatives were undertaken in parallel with regional diplomacy led by Secretary Kerry to better focus attention on the serious threat.

We finally sought to stabilize the Iraqi political process, recognizing that this attack took place at the most vulnerable moment, following national elections that were held on April 30 in which 14 million Iraqis voted, but prior to the formation of a new government. This process remains extremely challenging, but now has some traction. A new Speaker of Parliament was chosen last week. He is a moderate Sunni Arab named Salim Jabouri, elected with the overwhelming support from all major components in the new Iraqi Parliament.

Today, just about 2 hours ago, the new Iraqi Parliament elected Fuad Masum, a distinguished Kurdish statesman, to serve as the new President of Iraq. He, too, was elected overwhelmingly, with support from all major components in the newly elected Parliament. Iraqis are now proceeding along their constitutional timeline to choose a Prime Minister, which must happen within 15 days.

As the President has said, it is not the place of the United States to choose Iraq's leaders. It is clear, though, that only leaders who can govern with an inclusive agenda are going to be able to pull the country together and guide the Iraqi people through this crisis.

The current situation today in Iraq remains extremely, extremely, serious. ISIL remains in control of Mosul and it is targeting all Iraqis—Sunni, Shia, Christian, Kurds, Turkoman, Yazidi, Shaveks—who disagree with its twisted vision of a seventh century caliphate. It has also joined in an unholy alliance with militant wings of the former Baath Party, known as the Naqshbandi Network, and with some former insurgent groups, such as the Islamic Army of Iraq.

Going forward, the Iraqis, with our support, must seek to split these latter groups from ISIL and to isolate ISIL and the hard-core militant groups from the population. The platforms we have established through the immediate crisis response are now providing additional information to inform the President and our national security team as we develop options to protect our interests in Iraq.

Any further decisions in this regard will be made in full consultation with this committee and with the Congress.

Any efforts we take, moreover, must be in conjunction with Iraqi efforts to isolate ISIL from the population. This is because, while we have a serious counterterrorism challenge in Iraq, Iraq has a serious counterinsurgency challenge, and the two are inextricably linked.

Based on my last 7 weeks on the ground in Iraq, there is now a clear recognition by Iraqis from all communities that substantial reforms must be undertaken. This will require the formation of a new government, together with restructuring of the security services. An emerging consensus in Iraq, which we can fully support, is a functioning federalism consistent with Iraq's Constitution, based on the new realities on the ground, and focused on the following five principles.

First, local citizens must be in the lead in securing local areas.

Second, these local citizens defending their communities must be provided state benefits and state resources, perhaps modeled along the lines of a National Guard-type force structure.

Third, the Iraq Army must be restructured. Commanders who failed in Mosul have since been fired and they have been replaced with new commanders, who we are working very closely with. The federal army should also focus on federal functions, such as protecting borders, and rarely deploy inside cities, while providing overwatch support when necessary.

Fourth principle: There must be close cooperation between local, regional, and national security services to gradually reduce operational space for ISIL, particularly in Nineveh province.

And, finally, the Federal Government, through its new Parliament and a new Cabinet, must work diligently on a package of reforms that can address legitimate grievances from all communities and ensure adequate resources to these restructured security services.

These five principles can begin to address many of the core grievances in the Sunni majority areas of Iraq while also, importantly, denying space for ISIL to operate and thereby protect the Shia majority and other vulnerable groups from ISIL attack. Restoring stability and degrading ISIL will require a smart, integrated central, regional, and provincial approach led by a new Iraq Government, with an appropriate level of United States support and assistance.

Iraqi leaders from all communities have asked for assistance in implementing this program and General Austin, our Commander of CENTCOM, is on the ground today to further assess the situation and discuss concrete ways in which our assistance might be effective.

This model of a functioning federalism is achievable and it is essential if we hope to deny space for ISIL within the borders of Iraq.

I look forward once again to discussing more details in the answers to your questions, and I thank you again for the opportunity to testify this morning.

[The prepared statement of Mr. McGurk follows:]

Prepared Statement of Brett McGurk

Chairman Menendez, Ranking Member Corker, and members of the committee, thank you for inviting me to discuss the U.S. response to the crisis in Iraq. I just returned from Iraq after spending the past 7 weeks in Baghdad and Erbil helping to manage our crisis response with Ambassador Beecroft and our diplomatic and military team on the ground, which is serving with courage and dedication. We were assisted by the tireless efforts of Secretary Kerry, including a visit to Iraq at a critical moment, and the entire national security team, including the daily attention of the President and Vice President.

My testimony today will provide a firsthand account of the U.S. response In Iraq to date, and the foundations we are building to protect U.S. interests over the months ahead.

I. THE FALL OF MOSUL

I arrived in Erbil, the capital of the Kurdistan Region, on June 7, 3 days before Mosul fell to militants led by the Islamic State of Iraq and the Levant (ISIL). We had been concerned about Mosul for the past year, as it had become the primary financial hub for ISIL, generating nearly $12 million per month in revenues through extortion and smuggling rackets. From all of our contacts in Mosul, including Iraqi security and local officials, the city by day would appear normal, but at night, ISIL controlled the streets.

One of my first meetings in Erbil on the morning of June 8th was with the Governor of Ninewa province, Atheel Nujaifi. His news was alarming. Over the past 72 hours, he told me, hundreds of ISIL gun trucks, carrying fighters and heavy weapons, had crossed the Iraq-Syria border near the town of Rabiya, then passed north of Tal Afar, before staging on the outskirts of west Mosul. The Iraqi Army agreed to provide assistance to Mosul, but Iraqi commanders did not seem to appreciate the urgency of the situation, and stated that reinforcements might not arrive for a week.

We checked this information with sources in western Ninewa near the Syrian border crossings, and confirmed that ISIL appeared to be coming across in force. We also met immediately with Karim Sinjari, the Minister of Interior of the Kurdistan Regional Government (KRG), who confirmed with real-time information that neighborhoods in western Mosul were under immediate threat, as well as reports from the border regions about a steady stream of ISIL reinforcements crossing into Iraq from Syria. During this meeting, Minister Sinjari spoke to President Masoud Barzani and received authorization to deploy Kurdish Peshmerga units into eastern Mosul to help reinforce Iraqi Forces and deter any ISIL advance east across the Tigris. He said the Peshmerga were ready to help, but under the constitution, first required authority from the Government of Iraq.

We sent an immediate and urgent message to Baghdad, including to the Acting Minister of Defense, and directly to Prime Minister Maliki through his chief of staff. They responded that the situation was under control, and that nine Iraqi Army brigades would soon be relocated to Mosul. We questioned that information, and encouraged Baghdad to request assistance from Peshmerga forces immediately, as the Peshmerga was able to reinforce the city rapidly, and there was precedent for their helping to protect Mosul, including many years ago against ISIL's earlier incarnation, Al Qaeda in Iraq (AQI). The Minister of Defense ultimately agreed, but the Prime Minister asked for a confirmation from Erbil that any deployed Peshmerga units would withdraw after army units arrived.

On June 9, the situation remained static, and the Government in Iraq expressed confidence that Mosul was not under a serious threat. Throughout the day, however, Mosul's western-most neighborhoods began to fall to ISIL. Its fighters began attacking checkpoints and killing resisters, seeking to establish psychological dominance over Iraqi security units in the city. Together with the United Nations team in Baghdad, we worked to help establish a mechanism whereby Peshmerga units would be authorized to reinforce the eastern half of the city pending the arrival of Iraqi units from the south, and then withdraw after the situation stabilized. Baghdad asked to further review the proposal.

In the early morning hours of June 10, ISIL detonated a suicide truck bomb at a checkpoint across a strategic bridge and began to flow forces into the eastern side of the city. The next few hours would prove fateful. Iraqi units abandoned their posts, and ISIL swept through the city, seizing control of the provincial council building, the airport, and then, ultimately, Iraqi military bases. Nearly 500,000—out of a total population of 2 million Iraqis—fled, seeking refuge in Kurdish-controlled areas. Around 3 a.m., we received distressed messages from Iraqi officials in Baghdad, requesting the Kurdish Peshmerga to move into Mosul as soon as possible. The Iraqi request came too late.

The fall of Iraq's second-largest city to ISIL was combined with a social media campaign indicating that ISIL columns would soon be heading down the Tigris River Valley to Baghdad with no mercy for anyone who resisted. The result was a devastating collapse of the Iraqi Security Forces from Mosul to Tikrit. Nearly five Iraqi Army and Federal Police divisions (out of 18 total) would disintegrate over the next 48 hours. This snowballing effect immediately threatened Baghdad, with serious concern that Iraqi Forces guarding its northern approaches might also collapse.

Over the next 3 days, in meetings with our Embassy team and videoconferences with President Obama and the National Security Council, we immediately prepared and executed our crisis response. We also worked closely with Iraqi officials to organize the defenses of Baghdad and restore some of the confidence that had been battered.

II. U.S. RESPONSE

Our response to the immediate crisis proceeded along three parallel tracks. First, and most importantly, we worked to ensure the security of our own personnel and facilities. Second, in parallel, we both relocated and surged U.S. diplomatic, intelligence, and military resources to develop strategic options for the President with real-time and accurate information. Third, we worked with Iraqi officials to strengthen their defenses of strategic locations, and set the political process on track, with a focus on forming a new government following national elections.

The key elements of this response plan included the following eight steps, which, taken as a whole, encompassed security, intelligence, political, and diplomatic measures:

(1) Ensuring the Safety of U.S. Personnel and U.S. Citizens

Our first priority was ensuring the safety of U.S. personnel. This required relocating some personnel and adding additional security capabilities at the Embassy compound and the airport. Additionally, there were a number of American contractors at Balad Air Base working on Foreign Military Sales (FMS) cases. Reports from near Balad, which later proved false, suggested the base faced an imminent ISIL attack. After the contractors encountered delays securing their own charter aircraft, the Iraqi Air Force helped evacuate nearly 500 U.S. citizens and third-country nationals on June 14 aboard Iraqi C–130 aircraft. All contractors left safely, and we are grateful to the Iraqi Government and its pilots, most of whom we trained, for their assistance during this crisis period, particularly given their own competing demands.[1]

At the same time, we took extraordinary measures to ensure the safety of our Baghdad-based personnel. The entire National Security Council team, from the President on down, focused intensively to deploy Department of Defense security assets from elsewhere in the region while the Country Team worked intensively with Washington to relocate some personnel to safer areas. Within 72 hours we brought significant defensive capacity into our facilities and rebalanced staff to help manage the crisis. These early moves proved essential to ensuring that U.S. diplomats could continue to do their jobs and protect U.S. interests.

Today, even as the immediate crisis has passed, we are constantly reviewing our footprint to ensure the safety and security of our personnel and facilities.

(2) Improving Intelligence Picture on ISIL

Another immediate need was to get a better intelligence picture. From Erbil, even before Mosul fell, I was in touch with General Austin who recognized the urgency of the situation and prepared to deploy additional intelligence assets. In the earliest days, however, when asked about the situation, we had to acknowledge that we were operating in a fog. Rumors of ISIL convoys approaching Baghdad could not be discounted and there were tense moments as we sought to separate rumor and propaganda from fact without immediate eyes on the ground. Today, this fog has lifted—quite dramatically—thanks to immediate decisions taken by the President.

In response to these early developments, we dedicated a substantial amount of intelligence, surveillance, and reconnaissance assets to fly over Iraq. These missions have enhanced our intelligence picture and provided critical information to Iraqi Forces defending strategic locations, while at the same time helping to establish a foundation from which the President can assess the merit of additional measures.

(3) Assessing the Capabilities of the Iraqi Security Forces

In the early hours of the crisis, we worked quickly to reverse the collapsing morale of Iraqi Security Forces, reconstitute key units, and ensure the units deployed around Baghdad could adequately defend the capital. Our sight picture was imprecise, and the prerequisite to concrete action was acquiring a firsthand, eyes-on accounting of the situation. In my meetings with Iraqi officials, they said they would welcome U.S. Special Operations Forces to assess Iraqi force capabilities.

The President authorized the deployment of six Special Operations Forces "assessment teams" to augment efforts that were previously underway through our Office of Security Cooperation. These teams have recently completed an initial, 2-week assessment of Iraqi units in and around the greater Baghdad area, examining each unit's capabilities and potential for a closer U.S. partnership. This mission has already provided greater visibility into the situation on the ground, and will help the national security team calibrate additional and tailored measures.

The Department of Defense is currently reviewing this comprehensive assessment, which, as the President has said, is designed help determine "how we can best train, advise, and support Iraqi Security Forces going forward."

(4) Establishing Joint Operations Centers in Baghdad and Erbil

To harness an improving intelligence picture, we have stood up two combined Joint Operations Centers (JOCs) in Baghdad and Erbil. These JOCs help ensure a constant 24/7 flow of real-time intelligence information from across Iraq. We are now able to coordinate closely with Iraqi Security Forces, the Ministry of Defense, and the Baghdad Operations Center (BOC).

The Baghdad JOC is fully functional and has dramatically improved our ability to understand and assess the situation on the ground. I visited the JOC shortly before departing Baghdad last week, and it is an impressive operation, which began from scratch only 6 weeks ago. Most of our military personnel operating the facility have extensive experience and relationships inside Iraq. They report that their Iraqi counterparts have fully embraced our assistance and are asking for more, hoping that the United States will serve as their essential partner in the fight against ISIL.

The Government of Iraq has also made some welcome decisions in recent weeks to improve this bilateral coordination, including appointment of new commanders, many with longstanding ties and relationships with their U.S. military counterparts.

(5) Positioning U.S. Military Assets in the Region

In the immediate wake of the crisis, the Department of Defense reinforced assets in the region to prepare for multiple contingencies, including the possibility of targeted and precise military action against targets associated with ISIL. On June 16, Secretary Hagel ordered the USS *Mesa Verde,* carrying a complement of MV–22 Osprey tilt-rotor aircraft, into the gulf. Its presence added to that of other U.S. naval ships in the Gulf—including the aircraft carrier USS *George H.W. Bush,* a cruiser, and three destroyers. These assets will provide our senior leaders with additional options in the event military action is deemed necessary to protect U.S. interests as the situation develops. They also complement the substantial defensive capabilities now on the ground to ensure the safety and security of our personnel and facilities.

(6) Getting the Political Process on Track

ISIL attacked Mosul at a time of extreme political volatility. On April 30, 2 months before the crisis, Iraq conducted credible national elections, in which 62 percent of Iraq's eligible voters participated. This high turnout included Ninewa, where Mosul is the capital, with nearly 1.1 million voters turning out (54.4 percent), despite explicit ISIL threats to kill anyone who participates in the political process.

When ISIL moved in force into Mosul on June 10, the votes had been counted but not yet certified. The 4-year Parliament's term had ended, and a new Parliament, with 328 Members chosen in the election, had yet to convene. The attack, thus, took place during a political vacuum, and purposefully so. ISIL clearly took a play from its earlier incarnation, AQI, which led the devastating Samarra mosque attack shortly after December 2005 elections, triggering years of sectarian conflict. Their long-stated aim has always been to spark a collapse of the political process.[2]

We worked immediately to ensure ISIL could not succeed in destroying the Iraqi political process. First, we urged Iraq's Government to finalize the election results, which would set in place a series of timelines for forming a new government. This required judges who had fled Baghdad to return. They did so, and ratified the election, on June 16. The next day, Iraqi religious and political leaders from all major communities declared ISIL "an enemy of all Iraqis" and requested international assistance to combat the threat. Second, we worked with the U.N. to press Iraqi leaders to convene the Parliament on time, no later than July 1, which it did. Third, we pressed all newly elected political blocs to choose their leaders for key posts, pursuant to the constitutional timeline for forming a new government.

This process now has some traction. On July 15, the Parliament confirmed a new Speaker, which is the first position to be named pursuant to the constitutional steps required to form a new government. The moderate Sunni leader, Salim al-Jabouri, received votes from all major political blocs and was confirmed overwhelmingly, together with two deputies. The next step is confirming a President, which may happen as early as this coming week. Once there is a President, there will be a 15-day deadline to charge a Prime Minister nominee to form a government.

It is not the job of the United States to choose Iraq's leaders. We neither want to, nor have the power to do so. Iraq has a parliamentary system, and the next Prime Minister of Iraq must secure a 165-seat majority to form a new government. We do have an obligation, however, pursuant to our Strategic Framework Agreement, to "support and strengthen Iraq's democracy." Thus, from the moment this crisis began, we have actively prodded the process forward, serving as a neutral broker, and encouraging all Iraqi leaders to form a new government with leaders who reflect a broad national consensus between component communities.

The administration has been engaged on this issue from the outset, including the visit from Secretary Kerry to Baghdad on June 23, and to Erbil on June 24. The Secretary and the Vice President have also made regular phone calls to Iraqi leaders and to our regional partners to discuss the emerging situation and to help broker compromises where necessary to advance the political process and keep the system on track.

As President Obama has made clear, the Iraqi people deserve a government that represents the legitimate interests of all Iraqis. We are cautiously hopeful that Iraq's newly elected leaders are on their way to forming such a government, and as they do, they will find a committed partner in the United States.

(7) Building Regional Coalescence Against ISIL

At its root, ISIL is not strictly an Iraq problem. It is a regional and international problem. The Government of Iraq has requested international assistance, and it has stated clearly that it cannot manage this problem on its own, particularly with an open border and ISIL safe havens and staging areas in Syria. Accordingly, we have been regularly engaged with Iraq's neighbors and our key partners. The U.N. Security Council, European Union, Arab League, and NATO have strongly condemned ISIL's actions and expressed strong support for the people of Iraq.

Secretary Kerry's extensive trip to the region, capped by a quadrilateral meeting in Paris with the Foreign Ministers of Saudi Arabia, Jordan, and UAE, and then a visit to Riyadh for a meeting with King Abdullah, led to a new commonality of effort against ISIL. Shortly after Secretary Kerry visited Riyadh, Saudi Arabia pledged $500 million to U.N. relief agencies managing the humanitarian response in Iraq. In parallel, we are working with all of our regional partners to close down foreign fighter networks that continue to send thousands of terrorists into Syria, many of whom make their way to Iraq, with up to 50 per-month becoming suicide bombers.

We are also mindful of Iran's influence in Iraq and have seen Iran and Russia work to fill a security vacuum in the early weeks of the crisis. These activities are part of our daily conversations with Iraqi political and military officials, and we are confident that most Iraqi leaders want to retain strategic independence, while also grappling desperately with the serious threats to the Iraqi capital and the Iraqi people.

(8) Coordinating Humanitarian Relief Efforts and Protecting Religious Minorities

Finally, ISIL's advances have exacerbated a humanitarian crisis. The U.N. estimates that more than 1.2 million Iraqis have been displaced in fighting since ISIL moved into major cities in Anbar earlier this year. More than 300,000 Iraqis have fled to the Iraqi Kurdistan region since the fall of Mosul on June 10. We have praised the efforts of the Kurdistan Regional Government (KRG) in dealing with the situation, and call on the KRG to continue these efforts, as well as the Government of Iraq to assist the KRG with additional resources.

As noted, numerous countries have come forward and donated to the U.N.'s appeal for humanitarian assistance. In addition to Saudi Arabia, other contributors include Kuwait, Japan, New Zealand, and a number of others. The United States to date has contributed $13.8 million in humanitarian assistance in response to this crisis, and we are working closely with the U.N. team in Iraq to coordinate the response.

We are also particularly concerned about the state of the Christian community in Iraq, including in Mosul where this ancient community is being expelled by ISIL on threat of execution. There are now reports of the community's full scale departure, which saddens us deeply. We have also seen reporting of ISIL blinding and killing 13 Yezidi men when they refused to convert to Islam and the kidnapping of two Chaldean nuns and three teenage orphans in Mosul. We denounce these brutal actions vigorously. These actions by ISIL in Mosul—killing Christians, burning churches, killing moderate Sunnis, destroying Islamic tombs—prove to the world the barbarity of their objectives and why they must be stopped before their roots deepen.

Over the past 2 weeks alone, I met with the Christian leadership in Iraq, including Chaldean Patriarch Louis Raphael Sako in Baghdad, and Archbishop Bashar Warda in Erbil. I am always impressed by the deep faith and resilience of these leaders. In Baghdad, Patriarch Sako, shortly before my visit, presided over a mass with nearly 500 worshipers from across the capital. Both leaders also expressed detailed concerns about the plight of Christians in northern Iraq, and we are working with them and KRG leaders to ensure new Christian enclaves are protected and secured.

Finally, we are deeply troubled by ISIL's treatment of women as we receive a steady stream of reporting regarding women being deprived of their basic rights and subjected to gross violations of their freedom.

III. CURRENT SITUATION

It is now 7 weeks since this crisis began. Mosul remains in the hands of ISIL. Its leader, Abu Bakr al-Baghdadi, gave a sermon on July 4, at one of Mosul's oldest mosques, an act made possible after ISIL executed its moderate Imam and 13 other leading clerics in the city. The Iraq-Syria border, hundreds of miles between the Kurdish region and Jordan, is controlled on both sides by ISIL. Weapons and fighters now flow freely between Iraq and Syria, resupplying ISIL units fighting on both fronts. To say this situation is extremely serious would be an understatement. The situation is dire, and it presents a direct threat to all the Iraqi people, the region, and to U.S. interests.

Our immediate response, however, helped provide a barrier against further deterioration, and may offer a new foundation on which to begin fighting back. Since the first week of the crisis, the Iraqis—working closely with us—managed to absorb the shock, restore some morale, and began to push back, albeit with halting and uneven steps.

On the security front, an immediate focus was restoring control of portions of Highway One, which runs parallel to the Tigris River from Baghdad to Mosul. Iraqi Forces during the third week of the crisis managed to clear the highway from Baghdad to Samarra, ensuring a steady resupply for the historic shrine city. During the fourth week of the crisis, they cleared most of the highway from Samarra to Tikrit, although sophisticated IED emplacements, ISIL snipers, and repeated suicide attacks have halted progress.[3]

These operations remain extremely challenging, and we have differed with the Iraqis on some of their tactical objectives, such as moving into the city of Tikrit, which did not seem militarily essential given the need to focus on supply routes. They have, however, gradually allowed the Iraqis to move out of a defensive crouch and pressure the ISIL networks north of Baghdad, which had been poised to advance further to the south toward the capital. We are also urging the Iraqis to immediately focus security efforts to the west, where tribes continue to hold out against ISIL near Haditha, blunting what had been a rapid ISIL advance following the fall of Al Qaim, on the Syria border, on June 21.

The tribal situation in western and north-central Iraq remains fluid. Many tribes are now actively fighting ISIL—but lack the resources to do so effectively. According to our regular contacts in these areas ISIL is able to overmatch any lightly armed tribal force. The complete withdrawal of the Iraqi Army from these areas, together with the lack of coverage by Iraqi aviation in the border regions, provides ISIL free rein to move manpower and heavy weapons to areas where tribes resist.

The result has been many long-standing enemies of ISIL and its earlier incarnation AQI—such as Albu Mahal tribe in western Anbar; Shammar in western Ninewa; Obeidi south of Kirkuk; and Jabbouri in central Salah ad-Din—risk making accommodations to ISIL due primarily to the reality of battlefield dynamics. These tribes may have issues with the central government, but that alone is not why ISIL infiltrated their areas. In Al Qaim, for example, the Albu Mahal resisted ISIL for months, before the town ultimately fell after waves of attacks from across the Syrian border weakened Iraqi defense forces.

A tangible example of this dynamic is the Sunni town of Zowiya, near Tikrit in north-central Iraq. The residents there, a mix of Jabbouri and other tribes, resisted ISIL and would not accept their presence in the town. The result, as reported in the media and confirmed by our own contacts, was an ISIL military assault to kill all the residents of the village, starting with an hour-long artillery barrage. ISIL fighters then swept into the village, forcing surviving residents to flee, and sending the message to surrounding areas that any tribal resistance to their movement would be futile—and crushed.

As a result, absent some military pressure on ISIL, we are unlikely to see a broad-based tribal uprising against the movement, as happened between 2007 and 2008. This tribal uprising was enabled by U.S. military forces, which applied con- sistent and relentless pressure on then-AQI leadership networks, staging areas, and supply routes. While the Iraqis will never match this level of pressure, we must help enable their forces to better deny safe haven to ISIL within Iraqi territory. The Iraqis must also focus on training and equipping locally grown units to secure local areas. As the President said in his June 19 statement on the situation in Iraq, "the best and most effective response to a threat like ISIL will ultimately involve part-nerships where local forces, like Iraqis, take the lead."

The Iraqis recognize this principle, as well, and they have undertaken a reassess-ment of how their security forces are structured and might be reconstituted. Based on our most recent meetings with Iraqi security commanders, this effort will proceed in three phases. First, the Iraqis have begun to recall soldiers from dissolved units for retraining at two sites north of Baghdad. They report that nearly 10,000 have answered this call. Second, they are recruiting from existing units and from new volunteers for elite counterterrorism forces, similar to those we train through our Office of Security Cooperation. Third, they are looking to dramatically restructure their security services, with units recruited locally to secure local areas, while the national army provides overwatch support.

Such a program may take many months to demonstrate results, and years to pro-vide a lasting foundation for sustainable security. It will also be linked to the proc-ess of forming a new government, requiring a full national commitment and national resource base to ensure effective execution. It remains in our interest, together with such a national commitment from a new government, to provide appropriate assistance and help this process unfold in a manner that can eliminate space for ISIL over the long term.

IV. EMERGING WAY FORWARD—A FUNCTIONING FEDERALISM

The crisis response described above, together with Iraqi efforts over the past month, contain the elements of a longer term strategy to deny space for ISIL. Any such strategy, to be effective, must be deliberate, long term, and multifaceted. In my discussions with Iraqi leaders from all communities over the past 6 weeks, there is an emerging political-military approach that might begin to address the root causes of the current crisis.

First, it is important to focus at the outset on why this matters. The situation we confront is not simply about stabilizing Iraq, though that alone is an important interest. Rather, it is about ensuring that a movement with ambitions and capabili-ties greater than the al-Qaeda that we knew over the past decade does not grow permanent roots in the heart of the Middle East. Flush with thousands of foreign fighters and suicide bombers, ISIL in Syria and Iraq increasingly represents a seri-ous threat to U.S. interests.

Indeed, ISIL's leader, Abu Bakr al-Baghdadi, seeks to follow in the footsteps of Osama bin Laden as the leader of a global jihad, but with further reach—from his own terrorist state in the heart of the Middle East. After Osama bin Laden was killed in May 2011, Baghdadi eulogized his death and promised "violent retaliation." His audio messages routinely contain thinly veiled threats against the United States, and he has promised in a "message to the Americans" that "we will be in direct confrontation." The ISIL suicide bombers—still averaging 30 to 50 per month—are increasingly Western passport holders. Days ago, ISIL boasted that an Australian and a German blew themselves up in Baghdad, and it is a matter of time before these suicide bombers are directed elsewhere.

To combat this threat, we must proceed along three tracks. First, ISIL must be starved of resources, manpower, and foreign fighters. This requires working with our partners around the globe and especially with Turkey to seal the Syrian border from ISIL recruits. Second, the safe havens and training camps in Syria must be isolated and disrupted, preferably by the moderate opposition, enabled by U.S. training. Third, Iraqis must be enabled to control their sovereign space and reconsti-tute their western border with Syria, through capacity development, tribal engage-ment, and targeted military pressure.

This third element is essential, and achievable. It will require commitments from Iraq and support from the United States. Our perspectives may not always be the same, but our efforts must be mutually reinforcing. This is because, while ISIL presents a serious counterterrorism challenge to the United States, the Government of Iraq also faces a serious counterinsurgency challenge, and the two are inextricably linked. Our combined focus must be on isolating ISIL from the broader population and empowering tribes and other local actors to effectively combat it. This will require a combination of political and security measures, based on the principle of a "functioning federalism" as defined in the Iraqi Constitution—but never fully and effectively implemented.

In our view, a functioning federalism would empower local populations to secure their own areas with the full resources of the state in terms of benefits, salaries, and equipment. The national army, under this concept, would focus on securing international borders and providing overwatch support where necessary to combat hardened terrorist networks. Other critical reforms, such as an amnesty for those detained without trial, amendments to the criminal procedure laws, and addressing other legitimate grievances from the Iraqi people including those related to de-Ba'athification, will also be necessary elements to strengthen and empower local actors to stand and fight ISIL.[4]

While these concepts remain embryonic, and ultimately will require a new government to flesh out and develop, the five core principles can be summarized as follows:

1. Local citizens must be in the lead in securing local areas;
2. Local citizens defending their communities must be provided state benefits and resources (modeled along the lines of a National Guard type force structure);
3. The Iraqi Army will rarely deploy inside cities, but will remain outside in an overwatch posture and to carry out federal functions (such as protecting borders);
4. There must be close cooperation between local, regional (KRG), and national security services to gradually reduce operational space for ISIL;
5. The Federal Government must work diligently on a package of reforms that can address legitimate grievances and deny any pretext for ISIL activities.

These five principles can begin to address many of the core grievances in the Sunni-majority areas of Iraq, while also, importantly, denying space for ISIL to operate and thereby protect the Shia majority and other groups from ISIL attacks. Cooperation will be essential. The Government of Iraq from the center cannot restore stability in many areas that ISIL now controls, nor can local actors do so—without support and national-level resources—given ISIL's demonstrated capacity. Restoring stability and degrading ISIL will require a smart, integrated (central-regional-provincial) approach, led by a new Iraqi Government with an appropriate level of U.S. support and assistance.

Conclusion

The situation in Iraq remains extremely serious. While our immediate crisis response may have blunted the initial security crisis, ISIL represents a growing threat to U.S. interests in the region, local populations, and the homeland. Countering this threat will require close coordination between the administration and the Congress, and between the U.S. and our regional partners. I look forward to working closely with this committee to ensure that we are doing all we can to address this vital national security challenge.

Notes

[1] This cooperation is one of many examples of why it remains a vital interest for the United States to maintain our relationships with the Iraqi Security Forces, whether through our foreign military sales programs or training and advisory missions. The Iraqi Security Forces today face an existential threat, yet the quality of units varies widely from the highly proficient and professional to the incompetent and corrupt. The Iraqis recognize the serious work they must do to further professionalize the force, and they have asked for our assistance. It is in our interest to provide such assistance where we assess it can be effective, both to help confront the immediate crisis more effectively, and to build the long-term partnerships that are essential to maintaining strategic influence.

[2] The AQI attack on Samarra came at precisely the same moment in the political process as the 2014 ISIL move into Mosul: 2 months after national elections, after the expiration of full-term institutions, and before the selection of new leadership. The pace of signature AQI (now ISIL) attacks—measured by suicide and vehicle bombs—were also nearly identical in the months before the 2006 and 2010 elections, running at nearly 80 per month. In the 30 days prior to the April 2014 elections, ISIL launched over 50 suicide attacks inside Iraq with nearly all of the suicide bombers, according to our assessments and ISIL's own statements, foreign fighters who enter Iraq from Syria.

[3] During this period of crisis, Iraqi forces have increasingly relied on volunteers from southern Iraq to hold stretches of the highway cleared by security forces. Many of these volunteers have affiliations with Shia militia groups, and in the earliest weeks of the crisis, they operated in

the open for the first time in years. Since then, Grand Ayatollah Sistani has stated clearly that any volunteers should only join established state security services, and emphasized that militias or individual gunmen should not be accepted on the streets. The United States will continue to encourage Iraqi leaders to establish legal and practical mechanisms to incorporate volunteers, including tribal fighters, into the state security structures, where they can be trained to protect the population consistent with the rule of law.

[4] There are three fighting groups in the Sunni areas of Iraq. To be effective, any political-military initiative must focus on each of them. First, and most prominently, is ISIL. While there is no political solution to ISIL, political initiatives can help isolate ISIL from other associated groups. The second group is Jaysh al-Tariqa al-Naqshabandi (JRTN). JRTN is a militant wing of the former Ba'ath Party, now led by Saddam's former Vice President, Izzat al-Douri. While the most militant core of JRTN will remain nonresponsive to political initiatives, such initiatives can help minimize that core and degrade the network. The third group includes national insurgent movements, such as the Islamic Army, with some associated tribes. These groups mostly want local security control, and rarely launch offensive operations outside of their local areas. For them, there is a political solution, and through some of the reforms discussed above, these groups can probably be harnessed to protect local areas from ISIL infiltration over time.

The CHAIRMAN. Ms. Slotkin.

STATEMENT OF ELISSA SLOTKIN, PERFORMING THE DUTIES OF THE PRINCIPAL DEPUTY UNDER SECRETARY OF DEFENSE FOR POLICY, AND PRINCIPAL DEPUTY ASSISTANT SECRETARY OF DEFENSE FOR INTERNATIONAL SECURITY AFFAIRS, U.S. DEPARTMENT OF DEFENSE, WASHINGTON, DC

Ms. SLOTKIN. Thank you. Chairman Menendez, Ranking Member Corker, and distinguished members of the committee, I appreciate the opportunity to discuss the administration's response to the current security situation. My remarks will focus on what the Department of Defense is particularly doing.

I just want to foot-stomp some of the things that Brett just said. The United States does have a vital national security interest in ensuring that Iraq or any other country does not become a safe haven for terrorists who could threaten the United States homeland, our United States citizens, or our interests abroad.

As the President has said, ISIL's advance across Iraqi territory in recent weeks, and particularly its ability to establish safe haven in the region, poses a threat to United States interests and the Middle East. I do not restrict my views and my comments today just to Iraq, the geographic borders of Iraq. I do believe we have a real regional problem on our hands.

As Brett has said, the situation on the ground is complex and fluid. We are therefore taking a responsible, deliberate, and flexible approach to the crisis. But I do want to be clear: There is no exclusively military solution to the threat posed by ISIL. The Iraqis must do the heavy lifting. In the meantime, the Department of Defense remains postured should the President decide to use military force as part of a broader strategy.

Our immediate goals, as announced on June 19, are to: one, protect the people and property, our people and property in Iraq; two, to gain a better understanding of how we might train, advise, and support the Iraqi Security Forces should we decide to do that; and number three, to expand our understanding, particularly via intelligence, of ISIL. All three are critical to any future U.S. strategy vis-a-vis Iraq.

To that end, we have done four things in the Department of Defense. We have added forces to protect our people. The safety of our citizens obviously is our highest priority. The Department has met the requests of the Department of State. As described in the war powers notification we have transmitted, the Department of

Defense has sent what is called a Fleet Antiterrorism Security Team, what we call a FAST Team, a crisis response element, and additional military assets and personnel to reinforce security both at our diplomatic facilities in Baghdad and at the Baghdad International Airport.

The Secretary of Defense has also ordered the amphibious transport ship USS *Mesa Verde* into the Arabian Gulf. Its presence in the gulf is added to other naval ships, including the U.S. aircraft carrier USS *George H.W. Bush,* and provides the President additional options to protect American citizens and interests in Iraq should he choose to use them.

Number two, we have vastly increased our intelligence, surveillance, and reconnaissance, ISR, assets. At the request of the Government of Iraq, we have surged ISR over Iraq since the fall of Mosul and increased our information-sharing activities. These ISR sorties, which are up to 50-plus per day, give us a much better understanding of ISIL operations and disposition and allow us to help the ISF counter ISIL. We are now capable of around-the-clock coverage of Iraq and have been focusing our efforts on ISIL-controlled territory as well as Baghdad. We have also sent in U.S. assessment teams and stood up joint operations centers.

On June 19 the President announced these additional measures, including the deployment of just about 300 additional U.S. military advisers to evaluate how we might best train, advise, and support the ISF. These small teams of Special Forces are working to evaluate the ISF in and around Baghdad in particular. The teams are armed for self-defense, but they do not have an offensive mission. And then the two joint operations centers, one in Baghdad, one in Erbil in northern Iraq. They have both been established to help support our efforts on the ground.

A quick word about the assessments. I know that is of interest. Secretary Hagel and Chairman Dempsey received the draft assessment of the ISF last week from Central Command. Department leaders are undertaking a deliberate and rigorous review of the assessment, which will inform recommendations to the President. Meanwhile, additional assessment work continues. As you heard, General Austin is on the ground today with respect to the developing situation on the ground.

In closing, I just want to reiterate that we have a vital security interest in ensuring that Iraq or any other country not become a safe haven for terrorists. We do need a regional approach, and I look forward to answering your questions.

[The prepared statement of Ms. Slotkin follows:]

PREPARED STATEMENT OF ELISSA SLOTKIN

Chairman Menendez, Ranking Member Corker, and distinguished members of the committee, thank you for the opportunity to discuss the administration's response to the current security situation in Iraq. My remarks today will focus on two areas: (1) An overview of our national security interests in Iraq, and (2) a review of President Obama's current policy toward Iraq.

U.S. NATIONAL SECURITY INTERESTS

The U.S. has a vital national interest in ensuring that Iraq, or any other country, does not become a destabilized safe haven for terrorists who could threaten our homeland or U.S. interests and citizens abroad. As the President has said, ISIL's advance across Iraqi territory in recent weeks, and particularly its ability to continue to establish a safe haven in the region, poses a threat to both U.S. interests and the Middle East. In considering the ISIL threat, we don't restrict our view of the threat to specific geographic boundaries.

Despite this complex and fluid situation, we are taking a responsible, deliberate, and flexible approach to this crisis. I want to be clear that there is no exclusively military solution to the threats posed by ISIL in Iraq. However, DOD remains postured should the President decide to use military force as part of a broader strategy. Our immediate goals, as announced on June 19, are to (1) protect our people and property in Iraq; (2) gain a better understanding of how we might best train, advise, and support the Iraqi Security Forces (ISF) capabilities should we decide to support the ISF going forward; and (3) expand our understanding—particularly via intelligence—of ISIL. All three are critical to any future U.S. strategy vis-a-vis Iraq. To that end we have done the following four things.

Added Forces to Protect our People

First, we have added forces to protect U.S. personnel in Iraq. The safety of U.S. citizens and personnel in Baghdad and throughout Iraq is our highest priority. The Department of Defense is meeting all requests from the Department of State for security support to U.S. Embassy Baghdad. As described in the War Powers notifications we transmitted to Congress on June 16 and 26, DOD has sent a Fleet Antiterrorism Security Team (FAST), a Crisis Response Element (CRE), and additional military assets and personnel to reinforce security at our diplomatic facilities in Baghdad and the Baghdad International Airport.

Secretary of Defense Chuck Hagel also ordered the amphibious transport ship USS *Mesa Verde* into the Arabian Gulf. Its presence in the gulf adds to that of other U.S. naval ships—including the aircraft carrier USS *George HW Bush*—and provides the President additional options to protect American citizens and interests in Iraq, should he choose to use them.

Intelligence, Surveillance, and Reconnaissance (ISR)

Second, as part of this effort, we have surged intelligence, surveillance, and reconnaissance (ISR) capabilities in Iraq. At the request of the Government of Iraq, we surged ISR over Iraq after the fall of Mosul and also increased information-sharing initiatives. These ISR sorties provide us a better understanding of ISIL operations and disposition and allow us to help the ISF counter ISIL. We are now capable of around-the-clock coverage over Iraq and have been focusing our efforts on ISIL-controlled territory as well as Baghdad.

U.S. Assessment Teams and Joint Operations Centers (JOCs)

Third, we continue to assess the capabilities of the Iraqi Security Forces (ISF). On June 19, the President announced additional measures—including the deployment of up to 300 additional U.S. military advisors to evaluate how we might best train, advise, and support the ISF. These small teams of special forces are working to evaluate the Iraqi Security Forces in and around Baghdad. They are armed for self-defense—but do not have an offensive mission.

And fourth, following the President's direction, two Joint Operation Centers (JOCs), one in Baghdad and one in northern Iraq, have been established to help support our efforts on the ground.

The initial assessment mission is not unlike many others that DOD performs around the world. We currently maintain special operators in more than 70 countries, in Africa, the Americas, and Asia. Furthermore, since the U.S. troop drawdown in December 2011, a small presence of military personnel has been located at the Embassy in Baghdad, consistent with the 2008 Strategic Framework Agreement.

Secretary Hagel and Chairman Dempsey received the draft assessment of the ISF last week from Central Command. Department leaders are undertaking a deliberate and rigorous review of the assessment, which will inform recommendations to the President. Meanwhile, additional assessment work continues with respect to the developing situation on the ground.

In closing, I want to reiterate that there is no exclusively military solution to the threats posed by ISIL. However, we do have a vital security interest in ensuring that Iraq, nor any other country, becomes a safe haven for terrorists who could threaten our homeland or U.S. interests and citizens abroad.

The CHAIRMAN. Thank you.

Yesterday, during yesterday's hearing with the House Foreign Affairs Committee, you both argued that the policy of the United States should be for a unified Iraq with a strong Baghdad-based Federal Government. But many look and say that what is happening on the ground is accelerating toward a breakup of Iraq because too many of Iraq's communities no longer trust the Maliki government, and the question is whether there is anything we can do to prevent it.

Mr. MCGURK. Thank you, Mr. Chairman. I think we testified clearly and in my written statement, as well, that the model is a functioning federalism under the Iraqi Constitution. So nobody is trying to fit a square peg into a round hole that simply will not work. There is a model within the constitution for this functioning federalism, in which you recognize a very substantial devolution of authorities, the principles of local security control. That is something that I found in my last 7 weeks: there is an emerging consensus around.

Through the process of forming a new government, I think the details will be fleshed out. I know General Austin is discussing some of these concepts as we speak, particularly when it comes to restructuring the security forces.

So I do not think anyone is trying to create a strong central government that is going to retain control all over the country. In fact, I think everybody recognizes now that from the center out you are not going to be able to retain control in all parts of the country, but also, most importantly, locals and tribes on their own will not be able to deny space for ISIL, because of ISIL's very significant military capability. So you need a principle of local security control, but with a national resource base, and that is all within the federalist model of the constitution.

The CHAIRMAN. The question is, though, can you even get to a federalist model the way things are evolving in Iraq?

Mr. MCGURK. I think you can, because of——

The CHAIRMAN. What needs to happen?

Mr. MCGURK. Well, first we have to get a new government formed, and that is very important because the new government will obviously be the body that directs where the resources go.

The CHAIRMAN. What do we envision the timeframe of that being? It is past due, right?

Mr. MCGURK. Under the constitutional framework and the time lines, as soon as there is a new President, which just happened, there is now a 15-day timeline to charge a Prime Minister to form a government. So, we will know within 15 days the Prime Minister nominee. Whoever that is, he then has 30 days to name a Cabinet and present the Cabinet to Parliament for a vote.

Those timelines, however, can be substantially accelerated. For example, under the constitution, once there is a Speaker, there are 30 days to name a President. They did that in, I think, about 8 days. We are working very hard to accelerate those timelines.

The CHAIRMAN. Now, if it ends up being Prime Minister Maliki, how do you think that you keep this government together, this nation together?

Mr. McGurk. As I mentioned in my statement, as the President has said, it is not our job to pick the leaders, but the leaders do have to have a very inclusive agenda and pull the country together.

The Chairman. I am not asking you to pick, nor do I suggest we should. The question is that if that is the result by their own choice it seems to me that it is very difficult, based upon what has happened so far, based upon Sunni responses to ISIS, at least in the context of their grievances with the present national government, that—is not the likely outcome that we may see a divided Iraq?

Mr. McGurk. The Prime Minister will be chosen from the Shia political blocs, and Grand Ayatollah Sistani, interestingly, over the last month has been very active, and he has laid down some guideposts for how to form the next government: first, it has to correct the mistakes of the past, meaning it cannot look anything like the current government; second, you need new leaders that reflect a national consensus. We have had that now with the Speaker and the President, and so the Prime Minister will also have to reflect that emerging national consensus. It remains to be seen whether the existing Prime Minister could build such a consensus, but that remains very much in question.

The Chairman. You commented in the House hearing yesterday that options being developed for the President are more concrete and specific as a result of the U.S. military advisers on the ground and increased intelligence collection. What guidance have you received in terms of timing for these decisions and how will the political and security conditions on the ground influence the President's decisions?

Ms. Slotkin. Well, as I said, the assessments came in last week. They are dense, they are significant. So we are still working through those. After we have done that, the Secretary and the Chairman will make informed recommendations to the President.

The Chairman. Are you going to be able to tell us anything more than I read in the New York Times, which is more than I knew before you came here?

Ms. Slotkin. I understand. I would caution against using a leaked half-report in the New York Times as your basis for understanding it.

The Chairman. Well, the absence of having information leads me to only publicly reported resources. So when do you intend to come to us, in whatever setting, to advise the Congress? You know, this committee has jurisdiction over arms sales, and my reticence to arms sales to Iraq has in some respects been proven true when, in fact, we have had much of our equipment abandoned and now in the hands of ISIS.

So unless you are going to give us a sense of where the security forces are at moving forward, this Chair is not going to be willing to approve more arms sales so they can be abandoned to go to the hands of those who we are seriously concerned about in terms of our own national security interests.

Ms. Slotkin. Sir, I understand and our intent is to come and brief Congress at the time when we have piled through it ourselves. We have kept the Congress very informed. I know I have been up at least twice a week for our committees. We are committed to remaining in close contact with you and there is no attempt to hide it from you.

Mr. McGurk. I would just add, Mr. Chairman, that I think we are in a race against time, there is no question.

The Chairman. Well, that is my point.

Mr. McGurk. And one thing that we have found, first of all, by surging Special Forces teams, by surging intelligence assets, as you mentioned, we do know an awful lot more than we knew even 6 weeks ago.

Security forces around Baghdad and particularly north of Baghdad—I described this in some of my written testimony—are trying to do some things to fight back. They have taken nearly a thousand casualties in the last month. These units, particularly units that we have relationships with, are fighting, they are capable. And those are the types of units that we are looking at ways to further assist.

But again, this is all being discussed by the national security team.

The Chairman. Well, you have influences here. My understanding is Assad has been part of bombing ISIS in Iraq. Of course, you have Iran here. How is that going to complicate or instruct what you might be willing to do?

Mr. McGurk. It is part of the overall assessment, and I can only speak from my own firsthand experience in the initial days of this crisis as ISIL, it looked like, was moving down the Tigris Valley; our information was very sketchy, there was a bit of a panic throughout the Iraqi Security Forces, and we had to bolster them and try to create a circuit breaker so that that advance halted.

There was a security vacuum, that there is no question that our strategic competitors sought to step in and fill. Iraq lacks any capacity to do deep strikes in their border regions. Countries show up at their door and say, hey, we can help you with that. The Iraqis have pushed back in some regards, but in some respects they have accepted support.

The Chairman. They have accepted Assad bombing, have they not?

Mr. McGurk. No, no. We have no indication that there is any coordination with the Assad regime when it comes to security cooperation. But they are very concerned about the collapse of their border, particularly the collapse of Al-Qaim, which was a strategic border town which fell about 3 weeks ago.

The Chairman. They have accepted Iranian support?

Mr. McGurk. They have accepted low-level Iranian support; there is no question, yes.

The Chairman. Senator Corker.

Senator Corker. Thank you, Mr. Chairman.

Just along those lines, how do you assess U.S. influence right now? I know there are a number of other regional interests that are playing a role. I know that those of us who have visited recently know that before this all occurred U.S. influence was at an all-time low and really almost not present. I know that has changed some, but where would you assess our influence to be in Iraq right now?

Mr. McGURK. Senator, since this crisis, particularly in Mosul, we have been embraced, particularly our military personnel who have come in. I was at the joint operations center, which we have set up now. I was there on Thursday speaking with all of our military personnel there, all of whom have years of experience in relationships in Iraq. We have been embraced by their military, particularly the Special Forces assessment team.

The Iraqis have given us full access to their air space for our intelligence flights we want to do. They have given us the legal requirements we need to be there. So we have been embraced, and I think there is an opportunity because they certainly want our assistance. They want our equipment, they want our training. Our FMS package is about $15 billion total. They have paid about $11 billion of that. They put $193 million in the Federal Reserve into that account just last week.

So the Iraqis are very eager, under our strategic framework agreement, for U.S. assistance to be the backbone of their response. But, of course, there are things that they need to do as well and that is the conversation we are having with them.

Senator CORKER. Are there competing interests? I mean, as you are deepening the relationship again and helping in the way that we are, are there conflicts or competing interests that you are dealing with there on the ground?

Mr. McGURK. Yes, and in fact some of the tactics that the Iraqis pursue we totally do not agree with. In fact, I think by moving in aggressively as we have over the last 6 weeks, we will increasingly increase our influence over some of those tactics.

We have advised the Iraqis, for example, not go to into urban areas—lessons that we learned. The Iraqis made a decision to go into Tikrit. We did not really support that decision. We have advised the Iraqis since January not to go into Fallujah. They have not gone into Fallujah. But there is a military conversation, which is a little bit outside of my expertise and that is why General Austin is on the ground as we speak, talking to their new military commanders.

Just a point on our influence: I have had a number of conversations with the Prime Minister on down since January and have said: Your generals, Mr. Prime Minister, are not telling you the truth about the situation. That clearly was true, particularly in Mosul. Those commanders are now gone and they have appointed a series of new commanders, who we happen to work very closely with, and we hope that that type of relationship can continue.

Senator CORKER. I think that kind of involvement that we had and then we lost, where we were able to have the shuttle diplomacy and have the kind of activity that is now taking place, has helped create the situation that is on the ground, no doubt. On the other hand, Prime Minister Maliki has not been the kind of Prime Minister to create any kind of sense that a central government can resolve the ethnic and civil issues that exist there.

Do you really believe, bottom of your heart, there is somebody in Iraq of the Shia sect that can do that as Prime Minister if we move through this process?

Mr. McGURK. Senator, we have had extreme frustrations with the Iraqi Government, particularly over the last year, and that is one reason we have focused most decisively on making sure elections happen, they happen on time, and they were credible. And they did happen. They happened on April 30. They have created a new Parliament and through that Parliament new leaders will emerge.

There are a handful of very capable leaders who may emerge as the next Prime Minister of Iraq, but we are going to have to see. This will unfold fairly rapidly over the coming days.

Senator CORKER. Ms. Slotkin, I know there was a little discussion between you and the chairman relative to the assessment that is taking place. Can you just broadly tell us of anything that you have learned over the last 3 weeks that you did not know prior to the assessment?

Ms. SLOTKIN. Sure. I think the thing when we put the assessors on the ground that was the biggest open question, given the march ISIL had had across and into Mosul and down, was what was the status of Baghdad? Would the ISF be able to successfully defend Baghdad? That was our critical first question, especially given the size of our mission there.

I think one of the early things that we saw as we got on the ground was that there was a stiffening of the Iraqi Security Forces in and around Baghdad to protect the capital, which we thought was critically important. So we certainly were not aware until we got on the ground.

I do think some of the early indications are, frankly, mixed. There are some very capable units that have high morale and that are willing and capable of fighting, and there are other units where morale is lower, where there may not be as much capability and willingness to actually fight. It is sorting out the details of that that we are working on right now.

Senator CORKER. If you were to surmise after you do this assessment, what do you think the range of options will be that will be presented to the President relative to our activities militarily in Iraq?

Ms. SLOTKIN. I think, without crowding any decision space, all the military options we could possibly consider have to fit into a much wider regional strategy that is not a lead by the military.

Senator CORKER. Tell me what that means? I know you have said that in your opening comments.

Ms. SLOTKIN. Sure.

Senator CORKER. I think most people in this committee have been concerned. We had very, very strong support for efforts in Syria. Are you referring to Syria and Iraq? Is that basically the region?

Ms. SLOTKIN. It is Syria and Iraq, given ISIL's march. But then in particular it is making sure that we do not see a further spread. I mean, I know everyone was concerned——

Senator CORKER. Jordan.

Ms. SLOTKIN. Exactly. Jordan has been particularly a focus for us, given the border area right there with Iraq. But this is part of the administration's attempt to try and create this counterterrorism partnership fund to shore up particularly the neighbors of Iraq and Syria, to make sure that they have a flexible way to respond to the threats, to make sure we do not see that spread, and then to ask for funding for training the vetted Syrian moderate opposition so we have some sort of attempt from the inside of Syria to secure up those areas as well.

So it is impossible to just look at the ISIL threat at Iraq only because, as I said yesterday, it is kind of like air in a balloon; you squeeze on one end, it just goes somewhere else. We need a comprehensive approach outside in and inside out.

Senator CORKER. It is interesting you say that. I think people on this committee have been saying for like a year and a half that when the time was right, when we could have taken steps in Syria that could have prevented this, they were not taken. So now it is interesting that the administration is looking at a regional approach. Is that solely because now there is this counterterrorism issue, that the situation has gotten so bad—it did not have to, but it has gotten so bad now that it is a threat to the homeland and that is the reason you are looking at a regional approach?

What do you think it is that has taken so long, with so many people crying out on both sides of the aisle to, please do something relative to the moderate opposition in Syria, knowing that there is no border there, knowing that it was destabilizing Iraq? Is it this counterterrorism issue solely that has now caused the administration to look at it regionally?

Ms. SLOTKIN. I think the administration has been looking at this regionally for a while.

Senator CORKER. But it has been looking at it.

Ms. SLOTKIN. Well, I actually do not think that is fair. I think that we have invested heavily in some serious border security work with Jordan. We have done programs with Lebanon, we have done programs with Turkey. This is not beginning from anew here.

But I do think that the thing that surprised us, frankly, was the collapse of the Iraqi Security Forces in and around Mosul and four divisions essentially melting away. If you would have asked me that a year ago, I would have not assessed that. I think that the spread of ISIL, given the number of foreign passport holders that we know have traveled back and forth to Syria, Western passport holders, it does focus the mind.

Senator CORKER. If I could just ask one last question, or make a statement. We had a really, really strong vote here and a great debate on supporting the moderate opposition, and I was glad to get the call that the White House is now looking at I guess $500 million in actual Defense Department support for these moderates.

I have to say—and the first time I have said it out loud—I have now gotten to the point where I question—I hate to say it—how effective that is going to be at this point. I think there was a point in time when it could have been really effective. I now question whether now at this point, with all that has happened, knowing that ISIS has taken such a large part of the territory in Syria, I now question the effectiveness. And yet the administration really feels like that small amount at this late date still has the possibility to do real good in Syria.

Ms. SLOTKIN. Sir, I think you cannot fight something with nothing. So I think that it is important to start.

Senator CORKER. Well, we have been doing that for a long time. So it is interesting. So I agree with you and I think everybody here does. I guess the question is, can you fight something with almost nothing at this point, when it has festered into this type of situation?

The CHAIRMAN. And then we will have to move to Senator Boxer.

Ms. SLOTKIN. I do think it is important. We have put together a program that is scaleable. You can start small and move up significantly in the numbers and scale of the program, and we think it is critical that we start.

The CHAIRMAN. Senator Boxer.

Senator BOXER. Thank you.

I look at things just a little bit differently than a lot of folks here. I think the Iraqis had a chance of a lifetime and America's blood and treasure gave them that chance of a lifetime, a chance at unity, a chance at peace, and with their natural resources a chance at a growing economy. And clearly those of us, a minority of 23, who predicted this if we went to war, we did not prevail and that is life. You do not prevail, so you move on.

And then later when then-Senator Biden, who was the chairman of this committee, proposed more autonomy for the Sunnis and for the Kurds—and by the way—more than 70 Senators voted for that. The then-Bush administration laughed at it, kind of like people laugh right now. That is a lot of laughing. And that was turned away.

So the situation in Iraq I think is dire now, and I am not about to reinvest more lives and treasure. The United States has sacrificed too much. The war cost us $2 trillion. People predicted it would be over in weeks, months. More than 4,400 Americans were killed, their families never the same, 32,000 wounded during the course of the war. And we all know, and I praise Senators Sanders and McCain for battling to get help for those who are suffering from physical and mental injuries.

So I am pleased that President Obama said unequivocally "American Forces will not be returning to combat in Iraq," and I want to record to show that I will never vote to send more combat forces in. You know, you get so many chances in a lifetime.

I want to ask you about the Kurds, both of you. I do not know which one. Either of you could answer. The Kurds in northern Iraq have long been a strong ally of the United States, and they have played an important role in countering the rapid advance of ISIS. When I went to Iraq a very long time ago, the bullets were flying. The Kurds, I found them to get what this was all about.

There is so much prejudice against the Kurds. The Kurdish militia offered to support Iraqi Security Forces when ISIS began its offensive in Mosul. Kurdish forces have kept much of northern Iraq out of terrorist hands. Iraqi Kurdistan has become a destination for hundreds of thousands of Iraqis fleeing from ISIS-controlled territory.

I have to say, as I watch Mr. Maliki, I do not think he appreciates it. As the Iraqis continue to work to determine their future, I am asking you, what role can the Kurds continue to play, and should the United States acknowledge that the Kurds should have a significant amount of autonomy in a future Iraq? I think they have earned it, and I wondered what the administration's position is vis-a-vis the Kurds and more autonomy for the Kurds.

Mr. McGurk. Thank you, Senator. We are in a very active conversation with all the Kurdish leaders about their future. There are some realities that they are grappling with, the geostrategic realities and geographic realities, also their economic realities. They need about $14 billion to sustain themselves operationally. Their share of the budget this year, which is pending in Baghdad, is about $17 billion. We think there is a deal there within the constitutional framework that is in the best interests of the Kurds and also our interests both in northern Iraq and Iraq as a whole.

However, since this crisis began—and we recognize we are dealing with new realities on the ground that we have to recognize and deal with. We have established a joint operations center in Erbil to work with the Kurdish forces and with the Peshmerga to make sure, because they have about 1,000 kilometers now with ISIS on a good chunk of their border and they are going to need some help.

But that will work most effectively if it is done in cooperation and coordination with Baghdad, of course with us providing a mediating role where necessary. So we are in a very active conversation with them. They have a good deal of autonomy now and I am sure that they will ask for more through the government formation process, and that will all be done under the constitution.

President Barzani has been on the phone a number of times with our Vice President Biden to talk about these issues. Barzani has made it clear to us he wants to act through the constitutional framework for resolving some of the disputed boundaries in which the Peshmerga have moved by necessity over the last 6 weeks.

So the short answer to your question, we are in a very active conversation with the Kurds about this, and I am happy to follow up with you as it unfolds over the coming months.

Senator Boxer. And the United States will support more autonomy for the Kurds then, I assume?

Mr. McGurk. Well, through the government formation process there will be an active debate. I will just say we very much support the Kurds on particular critical issues. Baghdad about 4 or 5 months ago cut funding for salaries of workers in the Kurdish region. We have made very clear that is completely, totally, unacceptable and that has to be reversed.

The Kurds have also done some things in some cases in which we have said that might exacerbate tensions in a way that would not be particularly constructive. That is why we are in a very active conversation. But, we support autonomy within the constitutional framework, certainly.

Senator Boxer. I am just saying, I do not know what the future is of that constitutional framework, but we all hope it works.

The last question is: Are you confident we have adequate personnel on the ground to truly protect our Embassy and the Americans in Baghdad?

Mr. McGurk. Senator, yes. We have moved in substantial assets both to the airport and also into the Embassy. I was just there as late as Thursday and we are confident that our defensive perimeters and everything, that our people will be safe. Our Assistant Secretary for Diplomatic Security just visited Baghdad last week to do his own assessment and we have also had teams on the ground from CENTCOM. This is an ongoing assessment. And our intelligence assets have the entire, everything, all around the perimeter of the city of Baghdad, the airport, and our Embassy very well covered. So we are confident.

Senator BOXER. Can you tell us how many people we have at the Embassy, or is that something that you do not want to discuss in open session?

Mr. MCGURK. We have a total in Baghdad of about 2,500 now.

Senator BOXER. Thank you.

Thank you.

The CHAIRMAN. Senator Johnson.

Senator JOHNSON. Thank you, Mr. Chairman.

Mr. McGurk, let us quickly go back to the Kurds. I have been made aware of the fact that the Baghdad Government is basically in arrears on the Kurds' budget by about $6 billion. Is that pretty accurate?

Mr. MCGURK. There are a lot of ways to do the accounting and the math. Baghdad claims the Kurds owe them money, the Kurds claim that Baghdad owes them money, and in that space is where a deal lies. I think that is going to be part of the conversation in forming a new government.

Senator JOHNSON. If it is true that Baghdad owes them as much as $6 billion, would the United States support the Kurds' ability to export oil and obtain that revenue so they can keep themselves going?

Mr. MCGURK. We want to get as much oil onto international markets as possible from all parts of Iraq, and that is something that we very strongly support. We worked very hard over the last 6 months to get a deal on the table by which the Kurds would have exported as much oil as they possibly could through some of the existing arrangements, with the revenue-sharing allocations that exist. And that deal almost succeeded, but it ran up against the election timeframe, and once you had an election it was very difficult to close the deal.

But I think we will be able to get that back on the table. But we want as much oil from Iraq north to south onto international markets as soon as possible.

Senator JOHNSON. Now, I appreciate the fact that we are going through assessments and we are studying the problem. You have to recognize reality before you really develop a strategy. But, I really do want to just compare where we are now versus where we were prior to the 2007 surge.

Mr. McGurk, you have been involved in this for quite some time. What was the level of the Iraqi Forces back in 2007? I really want some relatively quick answers here because I want to get some data points.

Mr. MCGURK. How do you measure the level?

Senator JOHNSON. How many people were in the Iraqi Security Forces back in 2007?

Mr. MCGURK. I do not have the figure, but it was not a highly effective force in early 2007.

Senator JOHNSON. America, we had about 132,000 at the start of the surge and we surged to about 168,000, correct?

Mr. MCGURK. That is right.

Senator JOHNSON. What were we up against in terms of enemy fighters back in 2007?

Mr. MCGURK. We assess that the main enemy then was al-Qaeda in Iraq, which is ISIL. It is the same organization.

Senator JOHNSON. And about how many people were we up against?

Mr. MCGURK. These figures are always very difficult.

Senator JOHNSON. I understand.

Mr. MCGURK. We had assessments of 6 to 8,000 at the time, but probably more.

Senator JOHNSON. So what do we think current ISIL forces are?

Mr. MCGURK. Currently, the assessments we have seen—but again they are very difficult to measure—15,000 or so, in Iraq far less.

Senator JOHNSON. But basically double of what we had in 2007?

Mr. MCGURK. ISIL today, according to our assessments, is far more capable in manpower resources and fighting effectiveness than the AQI that we fought, yes.

Senator JOHNSON. That is my point. U.S. troop levels right now in Iraq are how many?

Mr. MCGURK. Total now about——

Ms. SLOTKIN. We have inserted 775 or so and we have about 100 that were associated with our Office of Security Cooperation.

Senator JOHNSON. So less than a thousand?

Ms. SLOTKIN. Less than a thousand.

Senator JOHNSON. Less than a thousand now. Back in 2007, prior to a pretty difficult battle, in terms of the surge, we had 168,000 at the height of that. And ISIL now is double the size that it was back in 2007 and they have some of our weapons; their capabilities are much higher.

Mr. MCGURK. That is right.

Senator JOHNSON. What was the size of the Iraqi military force in June 2014, prior to ISIL's move into Iraq? What was our estimate there?

Mr. MCGURK. I do not have that figure, but I can get it for you.

Senator JOHNSON. Are we talking hundreds of thousands?

Mr. MCGURK. Hundreds of thousands, but we try to look at capable and effective forces, and one of the purposes of the assessment was to determine which units are effective, which are ineffective. There are some units, quite frankly, that are totally ineffective and there are some units that are highly capable and effective.

Senator JOHNSON. Ms. Slotkin, do you have that information?

Ms. SLOTKIN. I think it is just shy of 200,000.

Senator JOHNSON. Two hundred thousand prior to the intrusion, the invasion?

Ms. SLOTKIN. I believe so.

Senator JOHNSON. How many now do you think there are? You said that they lost four divisions. How many would that represent that have just melted into the background?

Ms. SLOTKIN. Again, I do not have the exact number, but it is probably closer to 160-ish.

Senator JOHNSON. Do you have any sense of what percentage of that force would have any effectiveness in terms of fighting?

Mr. MCGURK. In terms of the dissolved units, it was about 30,000. The Iraqis have since recalled about 10,000 and, according to our OSCI assessments, there are about 10,000 who have come back and are going through about a 3-week training course now.

Senator JOHNSON. The effectiveness of the Iraqi Security Forces versus U.S. fighting forces? Not even comparable, right?

Mr. MCGURK. You cannot even compare them, no.

Senator JOHNSON. We have got a real problem on our hands.

We talked a little bit about the threat to our homeland that ISIL in Syria and Iraq represent. Can you describe what the threat to the homeland is because of the situation? Can you make the American people aware of why this matters?

Mr. MCGURK. What really concerns our counterterrorism experts and also concerns us is this rise in very dedicated global jihadist fighters coming from all over the world, many with Western passports. In Baghdad, just this week there was a suicide bomber. There was a German, there was an Australian. ISIL is able to funnel about 30 to 50 suicide bombers a month into Iraq. These are, we assess, almost all foreign fighters.

It would be very easy for ISIL to decide to funnel that cadre of dedicated suicide bombers, global jihadis, into other capitals around the region, or Europe or, worse, here. So that is a very significant, significant concern. They have training bases in Syria and they are recruiting on social media and the Internet, and it is something that we have never seen before.

Senator JOHNSON. A year ago the President declared the war on terror was over. Do you believe the war on terror is over?

Mr. MCGURK. I think we have a very significant fight on our hands with ISIL, which we have to manage.

Senator JOHNSON. I have no further questions.

The CHAIRMAN. Senator Cardin.

Senator CARDIN. Thank you, Mr. Chairman.

Let me thank both of you for your appearance here today and for your service to our country. I certainly agree that the United States has a vital interest in containing ISIS' growth and its threat to our homeland and to our allies. I also agree that we have a direct interest in dealing with a Government in Iraq that represents all the ethnic communities fairly with an effective government that gives confidence to moderates that their voices can be heard within the Iraqi Government.

But it was interesting. I was listening to Senator Johnson go through some of the comparisons on the strength of the terrorist networks. He was drawing a comparison over the last 7 years. But if you go back to before the U.S. troop invasion in 2001, at least my understanding was there was virtually no al-Qaeda, no terrorist network that was a direct threat to our homeland, in Iraq. So it does raise a lot of the questions that Senator Boxer raised initially, that our use of military force back in 2001 was ill-advised.

We do not want to repeat the mistakes that we have made in the past. That is the reason I bring it up. But I started with the fact that we have a vital interest in dealing with the current circumstances that are on the ground in Iraq.

I know this hearing is focused on Iraq, but I want to move a little bit to Syria and what impact ISIS is having on the opposition effectiveness in Syria and whether we are finding that any of the support for the opposition is strengthening ISIS' capacity within Iraq. The network between the moderate Gulf States and the opposition in Syria, are we confident that that equipment is not finding its way to the terrorist networks now operating in Iraq?

Ms. SLOTKIN. Obviously, the connection between ISIL—between the threat in Iraq and Syria is pretty significant. I do not personally know of any reports of opposition support then being funneled to ISIL. I think they are in a pretty bitter fight against both the regime and the terrorists, who have taken over territory particularly in eastern and northern Syria. So I do not have any reports of that equipment and that support that has been provided getting into their hands, but it is always a risk.

Senator CARDIN. What precautions have we taken with moderate Arab States and with our own support for the opposition in Syria to make sure that we are not finding American support or moderate Arab State support ending up encouraging terrorist activities now moving into Iraq?

Ms. SLOTKIN. This is something obviously we talk to our gulf partners about quite a bit, certainly over the period of the past couple of years, and we just urge them to make sure, similar to the way we do end use monitoring, that they have some way of telling who they are providing things to, in what capacity, et cetera, et cetera. We urge them to follow up the way we would want them to follow up.

Senator CARDIN. Mr. McGurk, how is the impasse in Syria, the failure to be able to have a workable plan in Syria, impacting stability in Iraq?

Mr. McGURK. It is a very good question, Senator. The Iraqis, since the beginning of the Syria crisis—and this is really all Iraqis—have had a different conception of the Syria crisis than we have had. They have been very concerned that, based upon their own experience, that were you to see the fall of the Assad regime, that it would unleash just chaos on their borders. And they take what is happening within that frame.

There is a Kurdish dimension to the Syria crisis. There is a central government in Iraq dimension to the Syria crisis. There is a tribal dimension to the Syria crisis. And it has just accelerated the centrifugal forces that are tearing at the fabric of Iraq. So it is very hard to even state the impact that the Syria crisis has had in Iraq, in particular the rise of the suicide bombings and car bombings, all of which we assess are ISIL. They come month after month and they are targeted—and this is ISIL's doctrine and ideology; you can go back to the writings of Zarqawi in 2004—to tear at the fabric of Iraq, to attack Shia civilians in their marketplaces, their playgrounds, their mosques, repeatedly, to attack Sunni tribal leaders who disagree with them. And that is why, in February, almost 86 percent of the suicide bombings that ISIL brought into Iraq were all focused on the Euphrates Valley and Anbar province, attacking Sunnis who disagreed with their ideology, and then to attack the Kurds in the disputed boundary territories in the north. That is what ISIL is trying to do.

We got that suicide bomber number down to about 5 to 10 a month in 2011–2012 and last year and this year it went up to 30 to 50 a month, and it has a devastating effect on the entire psychology of the country.

Senator CARDIN. Do we have any numbers on how many Iraqis have been displaced, either within Iraq or outside in other countries since June?

Mr. McGURK. Immediately, in Mosul there are about 500,000 IDP's, and since this crisis really started earlier this year, the IDP number is over a million.

Senator CARDIN. Are they in Iraq or are they in Iran or are they in other countries?

Mr. McGURK. Most of them are in Iraq and most of them have fled to the Kurdish region in the north. We have worked very closely with our regional partners and with our U.N. partners in Iraq to manage this crisis. Secretary Kerry, after he was in Baghdad, went to Paris to meet the Foreign Ministers of UAE, Saudi Arabia, and Jordan, and then went to Riyadh to see King Abdullah, and the Saudis right after that meeting very generously contributed $500 million to the U.N. agencies working in Iraq, which was a much-needed contribution.

We have contributed since the crisis began in Mosul, about $18 million, and we are working very closely, particularly with our Kurdish partners, to manage the crisis.

Senator CARDIN. I take it that very few of these people have returned because it is not safe at this moment?

Mr. McGURK. Yes, that is right.

Senator CARDIN. Thank you, Mr. Chairman.

Senator KAINE [presiding]. Thank you, Senator Cardin.

Senator Flake.

Senator FLAKE. Thank you, Mr. Chairman.

How long have we known that ISIL was a threat to the extent that they are now? How long has the State Department assessed it as a threat?

Mr. McGURK. We have known this organization since 2003. It is Zarqawi, Al Qaeda in Iraq. We have known it. We have watched it.

Senator FLAKE. I know we have known it, but at what point did we think that there was a threat that they would take over Mosul?

Mr. McGURK. Well, in Mosul they have had this modus vivendi in which they run racketeering schemes and they self-generate funding for about $12 million a month in Mosul. We have known that has been going on. Their open assault into Mosul, we did not have indications of that until a few days beforehand.

Senator FLAKE. Just a few days before that. When did we give warning to the Iraqi Government that this was a threat, or did they—has their intelligence network been sufficient to know this before it was a problem?

Mr. McGURK. It is a very good question, Senator. In fact, we have been giving warnings and expressing concern to the Iraqi Government about the security environment, not just in Mosul but in northern Ninewah, going back about the last year. And it was a part of the conversation that I know our Vice President had with Prime Minister Maliki, when Maliki was here in November.

We have been very concerned about it and are trying to work with the Kurds and with the Iraqi Security Forces in those areas to have some coordination, because ISIL comes through that border crossing south of a town called Rabia, and they have filled that space gradually over the last year.

Senator FLAKE. Without our military there actually conducting ground operations, our efforts have been in the diplomatic field, one, to try to convince the Iraqis to be more inclusive and to not give rise to this kind of activity or space for that kind of activity to happen, but, two, to warn them and help them combat this.

It seems to me we have been spectacularly unsuccessful in the diplomatic arena in that regard. Do you have any response to that? Or how hard are we working there? What intelligence do we have? Are we passing it on? Is the Iraqi Government simply unresponsive? What has been the issue here?

Mr. MCGURK. In terms of intelligence cooperation, sharing with Iraqi Forces and cooperation with Iraqi Forces, right now, as we speak, it is at a level we have not seen since our troops left in 2011. So there are some opportunities there for us.

Since we really started focusing on the al-Qaeda-ISIL threat in Iraq, really going back to last summer, you can see some statements that the State Department issued about Baghdadi, the fact that he is the leader of Al Qaeda in Iraq, he is now in Syria, and ISIL is an increasing threat to Iraq. We have developed platforms with the Iraqis to try to develop a better intelligence picture. But a lot of it was slow going.

On the political side, we were very focused when the crisis began in Anbar to make clear, very clear, that any tribal fighters rising up to fight this group will get full benefits and resources of the state. The Iraqis also agreed to train about 1,000 native Fallujans. They gave them 3 months of training and then they actually mobilized and there was an operation in northern Fallujah and, quite frankly, those fighters lost, and they lost because the ISIL networks, particularly in Fallujah, with snipers, with IED's, with their military sophistication, are able to overmatch any tribal force that comes to confront it. That is the situation right now.

It was also the situation in northern Ninewah, because we do have tribal contacts up there with the Shamar Tribe, which is the main tribe up there. And over time, given the infiltrations from Syria, given the amount of force that ISIL can bring to bear, it was very difficult for locals to stand up to them.

Senator FLAKE. You say cooperation with the Iraqi Government was slow in coming. Where does the fault lie with that? Were we slow to recognize the threat of ISIS or was the Iraqi Government simply slow to heed the warnings that we were giving or the cooperation that we offered?

Mr. MCGURK. I think we started moving fairly aggressively in the summer. The Iraqis wanted to do things on their own. They did not really formally request direct U.S. military assistance until May, although there was a conversation about the possibility of such assistance earlier than May. But the formal request came in May.

The Iraqis are very proud of their sovereignty. We have a strategic framework agreement with them, which allows us to do an awful lot. But the notion of flying surveillance drones over Iraqi skies, quite frankly, was something that was controversial at first.

So we had to develop the mechanisms and the procedures for doing these things, and we have those now well in place.

Senator FLAKE. Our role in Congress, one of our main roles, obviously is to provide funding for these conflicts, for intelligence, for diplomatic efforts. Aside from thousands of lives lost, we have spent about $800 billion at last count in Iraq, just in Iraq. What can we tell our constituents that we have gotten out of that? Where are we now that we would not be had we not spent $800 billion?

Ms. SLOTKIN. I think, as Senator Boxer said, we gave them an opportunity and we hope that this is not the end of the story in Iraq. We believe that there is still an opportunity for the Iraqis to form a government and do something about this problem, and we are urging them to get on with it.

I think that we still believe in a way forward in Iraq. They just have to take the opportunity.

Senator FLAKE. Is it possible at all in the State Department's view to move ahead with Maliki in charge? Will there be sufficient trust, any trust, in the Sunni population that he will be inclusive enough, his government? Or does our strategy rely on somebody else coming in?

Mr. MCGURK. Again, it is going to be very difficult for him to form a government, and so they are facing that question now, now that the President has been elected, to face the question of the Prime Minister. Any Prime Minister, in order to form a government, is going to have to pull the country together. So whoever the leader is is someone that is going to have to demonstrate that, just to get the votes he needs to remain or to be sworn into office.

So that is something that is going to evolve fairly rapidly over the coming days. Again, there is a 15-day timeline to nominate a Prime Minister, and then whoever the nominee is still has to then form a Cabinet and present it to the Parliament to form a government.

The Speaker of the Parliament, again, was elected overwhelmingly with support from all major groups, as was the President, and we would anticipate the Prime Minister. As we have said, as the President has said, it has to be somebody that has a very inclusive agenda and that can bring all the component groups together. Otherwise he will not be able to govern.

Senator FLAKE. Thank you, Mr. Chairman.

Senator KAINE. Thank you, Senator Flake.

Senator Coons.

Senator COONS. Thank you. I want to thank Senator Menendez for chairing this hearing, and Senator Kaine and Senator Corker for your leadership on this committee as well, and thank our witnesses for your testimony today. I will follow on Senator Flake's questioning in a moment.

I share the administration's ultimate goal as you have just been testifying to of encouraging the creation of an inclusive Iraqi Government that is supported by all of Iraq's different sectarian groups, that has some hope of a secure and stable Iraq going forward, given how much has been sacrificed over how many years.

But I will also renew a theme you have heard from several Senators, that I do not support a return of active U.S. combat troop presence in Iraq. I am concerned about the security of our Embassy and our personnel and I am very concerned about the region and about some of our vital regional allies. So first I think we do need to deal with defeating ISIS and the regional threat here in the regional context, as you testified. And I think it is imperative that we have to find a way to move forward that has some reasonable chance of resolving the ongoing crisis in both Iraq and Syria to the best interests of the United States, of Israel, of Jordan, of Turkey, of all of our regional allies.

First, on the point you were just discussing, what do you see as the prospects, the path forward for a political solution here in these next 15 days? Have you met with anyone who strikes you as a promising potential Prime Minister, who really could bridge these divides? Given reports of high-level delegations of Iranian military officials and diplomats meeting in Baghdad and in Najaf, I am concerned that there are fewer and fewer realistic chances of a broad-based, inclusive government being formed, given active interference and engagement from Iran.

Mr. McGURK. I can speak a little bit to the process. This was Iraq's third national election they held on April 30. It was one of the best elections they have held in terms of the turnout. In 2006 it took about 7 months to form a government and was an extremely difficult process, and what they did was they built this very bloated government with every seat filled and then voted it into office. In 2010 it wound up being the same thing. It took 9 months, and again they built a very bloated structure and then swore it into office.

This year, this time, they are proceeding quite differently. They are moving through their constitutional timeline: Speaker, President, now Prime Minister. It is moving much faster than ever before. Nine months in 2010. We are less than 3 months out from the April elections and we are now on the step for the prime ministership.

I would be hesitant to put timelines on it because it is a very complicated process. The 328 members in the Iraqi Parliament represent the entire spectrum of political thought in Iraq, and so it is very difficult to get full unity on any one person or any one issue. So there will be a very strong debate. It is not beanbag, the political process there. Now they are starting to focus on the most critical question of who is going to lead the coiunty as the chief executive.

Senator COONS. Your riveting description of the fall of Mosul suggests that a lack of urgency, a lack of reality, about the situation on the ground was outcome determinative, led to a failure to act in a timely way and to ISIS sweeping across much of the center of the country. Do you think there is a sense of urgency, a sense of reality, both as to the defense posture that ISF now faces and to the political challenges that they face?

Mr. McGURK. Yes. There is a culture in Iraq that sometimes folks do not want to give their leaders bad news, and sometimes we are the ones who have to deliver the bad news and say ''you face a very urgent situation.'' Mosul was a good example of that. The generals up there were not saying that it was particularly urgent. So we are often the ones that have to do that.

Now, given the information we have, given the relationships we have on the ground, military relationships, we are able to give them a very clear picture of the situation they face. The relative tactical success they have had in clearing some of the highways north of Baghdad—and relative because it remains very difficult, but the highway—it is Highway 1 that goes all the way, up north through the Tigris Valley from Baghdad to Samarra. They did clear that. That was partially on their own, but partially because we helped them with some information. Then, the next stretch, from Samarra to Tikrit, the same thing. As I mentioned, we did not advise them to go into Tikrit City itself because that is a very difficult military environment to operate in.

But, again, that is why General Austin is on the ground, to discuss with their new commanders, who we have very good relationships with, and with the Iraqi political leaders, how we can better approach this going forward in a more cooperative way.

Senator COONS. Ms. Slotkin, there has been widespread reports of Sunnis sort of bristling under ISIS rule. They are extreme, they conduct not just terror attacks and suicide bombings and targeted assassinations, but they also are imposing a particularly harsh form of sharia. What prospects are there for outreach, for reengagement with elements of the Sunni community that might assist the Iraqi Security Forces, might play some role in rising up against ISIS in a replay of what happened previously?

Ms. SLOTKIN. I think we have seen this story before in our own experience in Iraq, that many of these groups who may give tacit support to terrorist organizations in their neighborhoods, as soon as there is some prospect of turning against them and they know they have some support from their central government to do it, then they will turn on them. They do not like living under sometimes the sharia law that has been imposed on them.

So I think the prospects are still there. But I think ultimately it will come down to whether they feel like they have a partner in the central government of Iraq, there is something to break away for. And that is up to the Iraqi Government. The new government will have to attract the Sunnis away from ISIS and ISIL and toward them. The security forces have to be a part of that, but at the end of the day it is about a political compromise that they strike in Baghdad and lure those Sunnis away.

Senator COONS. I am particularly concerned about our vital ally in the region Jordan, about their both military and economic and strategic stability, given the flood of refugees that they have already been taking in as a result of the Syrian crisis, and about the open, increasingly porous borders. What concrete steps are we taking to reinforce and to ensure the stability and vibrancy of Jordan, and how does the announced intent to deliver support to the vetted moderate Syrian resistance strengthen that?

Ms. SLOTKIN. I think the most important thing is that the Jordanian military is a very capable military force. So we are very focused on the threat right on their border, but so are they. They have reinforced their troops on their border with Iraq, and we have a very close relationship, military to military relationship, with the Jordanians and talk with them on a daily basis.

Again, because of the Syria crisis the United States already had a robust presence in the country. We have F–16's there, we have a Patriot battery there. We have a $300 million FMF program. We do education with them. It is a strong relationship, one of the strongest in the region. So I feel confident that we are doing everything we can in response to any request that they have to help them with their situation on the border.

I think the idea of supporting moderate, vetted opposition in Syria is only more positive. The United States needs capable partners and platforms in the region to deal with this very fluid threat. The Jordanians are a big part of that and so will the Syrian moderate opposition.

Senator COONS. Thank you.

Thank you, Mr. Chairman.

Senator KAINE. Thank you, Senator Coons.

Senator Risch defers his questioning for now to Senator Rubio.

Senator RUBIO. Thank you. I appreciate that.

Let me begin with my—I think our priority for everyone here is the safety and security of our personnel, including Department of Defense personnel and certainly the State Department personnel at the embassy, given recent events. So there has been increased reporting that the ISF is increasingly linked or intermingled with Shia militia forces, that some of these Shia militia forces are actually now wearing ISF uniforms, but it is becoming increasingly difficult to distinguish between a Shia militia fighter and an ISF personnel.

We have seen open source reporting that the Shia militia could pose a threat to our personnel, including potentially our military trainers and others. Can you briefly describe, number one, how we assess the threat of these militia and what are we doing to mitigate the risks that they could pose to our personnel, given the fact that they are now basically embedded and intermingled with the Iraqi Security Force personnel that we are working side by side potentially with?

Ms. SLOTKIN. Sure. This is exactly what we were trying to assess by going over there and looking unit by unit in and around Baghdad at things like command and control, morale, and in particular infiltration of Shia militias. Grand Ayatollah Sistani put out a very public call for volunteers to join the military, so one thing we watched very closely was as all these new folks came in where would their allegiances be? Would they respond to the commanders of their unit or someone else?

I think that is what we have been trying to figure out, and I think the picture, honestly, is mixed. In some areas we have good morale, strong adherence to command and control through the military channels, and in other places it is more of an open question. Those are the kinds of units that we do not want to be working with and why we are taking this very sort of deliberate approach.

Senator RUBIO. Well, but there is the real risk, is there not, that Shia militia that are there could just as easily be the ones firing on our Embassy and on our personnel as ISIL personnel could be, unless they are somehow otherwise constrained?

Mr. MCGURK. Senator, the Shia militias are something we watch very closely. There has been a cease-fire. The Shia militias have had a cease-fire in place since 2009 against their own government forces, a cease-fire. We have not had any attacks from Shia militias since 2011. But it is something that we watch extremely closely.

The assessment assessed every unit around Baghdad and, without getting into the details, some units are infiltrated and dangerous. Some of them, however, are very capable, very effective, and have close relationships with us.

Senator RUBIO. I wanted to get to a broader question, and you touched upon it in your statement and you do even more so in the written statement that you have submitted. But here is the question that we get from people, and that is people are outraged by what is happening, especially the reports coming out about the different things that ISIL is doing. By no means is this a group that is popular and I think Americans understand this is a terrible, radical group of violent individuals.

That being said, public opinion polls and just from the phone calls we get in our offices, the attitude of much of the American public is it is a mess, but it is their problem, let them figure it out. I have personally said that this is not even about Iraq at this point; it is about the long-term security of the United States, and that the threat that ISIL poses to the United States, especially if they are able to establish a safe haven of operations similar to what al-Qaeda did, in fact, even worse than what al-Qaeda was able to do in Afghanistan.

But I was hoping that from the administration's point of view and from the State Department and the Department of Defense's point of view you could perhaps use this as an opportunity to explain to my constituents in Florida why this matters to America, why something happening halfway around the world, in a country that people, quite frankly, think increasingly perhaps we should not have gotten involved in? Why does this matter? Why should people care about what is happening in Iraq, given the problems we have here at home?

Mr. MCGURK. Thank you, Senator. Let me say a couple of things. I, of course, address the ISIL threat in my written and opening statement, and that is a very serious counterterrorism threat, and that is number one.

But these are vital, vita,l United States interests in Iraq. Number one: the counterterrorism, the al-Qaeda threat. Number two: just the supply of energy resources to global markets. Iraq through 2035 will account for 45 percent of all of the growth in oil energy exports. If Iraq were to collapse in a major civil war and sectarian war, the effects to our own economy here at home would be quite serious.

Every single faultline crossing through the Middle East—Arab-Persian, moderate, extremist, Shia-Sunni, Arab-Kurd—everything meets in Iraq. So were ISIL to get into, for example, the mosque city of Samarra, which it wanted to do, and to unleash a cauldron of sectarian violence, it would spread throughout the Middle East, with devastating effects for our economy here at home.

So vital interests, from al-Qaeda to energy resources and our own economy, are at stake.

Senator RUBIO. Thank you.

Did you want to add something?

Ms. SLOTKIN. I would just foot-stomp the ISIL threat. They are self-funded. They have control of significant territory. They are tested in battle. They are a serious threat. And while we do not assess right now that they are doing distinct homeland plotting, they have certainly said rhetorically—they are open about it—that they are coming for the United States.

In my experience as a Defense official, I do not want that to fester. I want to do something about that.

Senator RUBIO. I thank you for that. I think you have done a good job of outlining the reason why we should care and why this matters. This is not simply about Iraq. This is about the United States.

Could you then briefly—if I brought some people in here from Florida or they are watching or I were to share this video, could you explain to them what our plan is? What are we doing? What are the two or three things that we are doing to address this threat, which as you have described is a very significant one to our country? What is the plan?

Mr. MCGURK. Let me focus on ISIL. We need to do three things. We need to strangle their entire network. That means their foreign fighter flow in particular. We just had a meeting all day yesterday with the Turks to focus on that. We have to strangle their foreign fighter flow network into Syria.

Number two, we have to begin to deny space and safe haven and sanctuary, which they have in Syria, which gets into why we are training, planning on, hoping to train the moderate opposition with a train and equip program.

Number three, we have to help the Iraqis take control of their sovereign space. To do that, as I explained in my testimony, a functioning federal system in which we do recruit locally, with local tribal structures, but with the resources of the central government, because there was a conversation about recruiting tribes, which is what we want to do. But we have to recognize that unless the local people and local tribes have the resources of the central government or national-based resources, they are not going to be able to defeat this organization.

Senator RUBIO. What are we specifically doing and going to be doing to crush their networks and prevent them from having safe havens? Operationally, what are we going to do to accomplish those goals that you have outlined as part of our plan?

Mr. MCGURK. Well, I can speak to the Iraq portion of this, and this is why, since this crisis began in early June, we immediately surged in a significant surge of intelligence assets into Iraq, to get a better picture of the situation. We put special forces on the ground to get eyes on. We are now at the point where we have collected all the information and we have a fairly concrete, precise, picture and we are coming up with options for doing just that. So this will be an ongoing conversation with this committee and the Congress over the days and weeks ahead.

The CHAIRMAN [presiding]. Senator Shaheen.

Senator SHAHEEN. Thank you, Mr. Chairman.

Thank you all for being here. I want to follow up a little bit on the line of questioning that Senator Rubio was following and your response, because you mentioned in your testimony, Mr. McGurk, that we need to work with our partners in the region, especially Turkey, to seal the border to Syria from foreign fighters and ISL recruits. So can you talk a little bit more—I know you are limited to some extent—about how this is proceeding and what other partners we might engage to address this concern?

Mr. McGurk. Thank you, Senator. We have some experience in doing this in the late 2006, 2007 timeframe, where it was the same foreign fighter network. At the time they were all flying into Damascus, going to Aleppo, and following a rat line into Iraq. We squeezed it. We did an anaconda strategy to squeeze the entire network from the source capitals, where they were getting on airplanes, to get them off the airplanes.

We are now doing a similar effort, and Ambassador Bradtke is Senior Adviser at the State Department under the CT Bureau, focused on the foreign fighter network. It is two parts: Turkey has a very long border. It is very hard to control. Turkey is doing some things to strengthen its own border and focus on this problem; also, the source capitals in which young military-age males are getting on airplanes and going to certain airports in Turkey.

So we are working very carefully through our entire interagency and the folks that are really expert in this, with the source capitals in which people are getting on airplanes and coming into Syria, and with the Turks. It is Europe, it is North Africa, and it is the gulf region.

Senator Shaheen. Can you talk about how long we have been doing that and whether we are seeing any results as a result of that effort?

Mr. McGurk. Senator, we have been doing it for some time now. I can follow up with you after speaking with the experts dealing with this and have a written response.

Senator Shaheen. I would appreciate that, and probably sharing it with the committee would be very helpful as well.

You also talk about the tremendous effort on the part of the Kurdistan government to accommodate the internally displaced people fleeing from other parts of Iraq. I wonder if you could talk about the extent to which the Government in Baghdad recognizes the strain this is causing and has been willing to work with the Kurds at all to help address this.

Mr. McGurk. One promising sign, Senator, in what is a very dark landscape—I want to be very clear. This humanitarian situation is extremely serious and it is heartbreaking, particularly when it comes to the Christian minorities and other vulnerable groups. I met with the Christian leadership in Erbil and Baghdad, throughout my last trip, about how we can do a better job helping these people, who are under a very serious threat.

The Iraqi Government could do more to help the Kurdish Regional Government, particularly with state resources and state funding. The Iraqi Parliament, which is just meeting because it just convened for the first time, it is a brand-new Parliament. It has a brand-new Speaker. The first session really was yesterday, and one of the first things they did, first they all united in condemnation of what is happening to Christians in northern Nineveh province. And they also formed a very broad committee from all the major groups to figure out how to direct state resources—and, remember, Iraq has significant resources. There is a budget pending in the Parliament for $140 billion, and that is something that the government has to tap into to help these people.

So they just formed a committee yesterday to figure out some things to do, and we are obviously actively engaged with them to try to influence that process.

Senator SHAHEEN. So does the selection of a Kurdish President help with this effort?

Mr. MCGURK. Certainly. We look forward to working with the new President, with President Fuad Masum, on these issues. Again, he won an overwhelming victory on the vote today on the floor of the Iraqi Parliament. So it is a good step forward. But we work with all the Kurdish leadership in Erbil and Sulaymaniyah, and also in Baghdad.

Senator SHAHEEN. But I would assume that, given his election, that he might have some influence in the Parliament that could be very helpful. Has he made statements about the need to help address what has happened to Christians?

Mr. MCGURK. Well, he was just elected as I was coming over here in the car. So I have not seen the statements that he has made yet. But we will be immediately working with him and, again, all the leaders to get the resources up to the north that the Kurds need to deal with the humanitarian crisis.

Senator SHAHEEN. Finally, again I think this is for you, Mr. McGurk, but, Ms. Slotkin, if you would like to weigh in, please do. One of the things that has not gotten a whole lot of attention, but has—you mention it in your testimony and certainly we have seen it in other places where extremist Islam has been in charge—the plight of Iraqi women and girls has borne the brunt of a lot of the violence as they have advanced through Iraq.

Can you talk about what we can do and what is being done to help address this?

Mr. MCGURK. Well, first, Senator, the fact that you are asking the question is number one, because we have to put international focus and attention on this very serious problem. In Mosul the situation with ISIL goes from bad to worst. They have first gone after the Christians, then they have gone after Kurds. They are now going after women and, particularly, young women.

This is a serious international problem. The Government of Iraq, the Foreign Minister of Iraq, wrote a letter to the Secretary General of the United Nations asking for international assistance against this threat to their people. So it is something that we need the entire efforts of the entire world to focus on, because, frankly, the Iraqis cannot deal with it on their own.

So, first we have to give it international attention. Then we have to find a way to really address it. But in my testimony, particularly in Mosul, where ISIL is setting up really its capital of its caliphate—that is what it is trying to do—we have to find a way to work effectively with local tribal forces to be able to make sure that they can stand effectively against ISIL, which right now, frankly, they cannot, and the Kurdish Peshmerga forces, because Mosul is in a pocket in the Kurdish region, and eventually federal forces, to be able to slowly squeeze and take back these areas.

This is going to be a long-term effort, but, especially for the sake of the people living in these areas, we have to give it everything we have.

Senator SHAHEEN. Finally, I am almost out of time, but this may have been asked and I apologize if you have already answered it. But there was a report in the New York Times on July 13 that suggested that only about half of Iraq's operational units are capable enough for us to advise them. Can either of you speak to whether—without revealing classified information—whether we are concerned about this, the substance of this report being accurate?

Ms. SLOTKIN. Sure. It was mentioned briefly and I just cautioned against relying solely on a leak in the New York Times. That was a critical thing that we were looking at in these assessments. They are still in draft. I think what is accurate is that the picture is mixed. I do not know if it is exactly half, but I think that we are finding units where that is a real problem and units where it is not a problem.

And we are trying to understand how to process that. What does it mean if certain units we can work with and they are ambitious and they want to do things to take back their territory and others are not the right units for us to be working with. What should our policy be in that case? That is complicated and that is why we are taking our time to think about it.

Senator SHAHEEN. Thank you.

Thank you, Mr. Chairman.

The CHAIRMAN. Senator McCain.

Senator MCCAIN. Thank you, Mr. Chairman.

Ms. Slotkin, we learn more from the New York Times and from the Wall Street Journal than we do from any briefing that we have ever had with you. I do not agree with you very often, but I certainly do agree with your statement you cannot fight something with nothing, because that is what we have been doing, nothing.

This situation in Iraq was predicted by us and predictable, and now we find ourselves in a situation where, Mr. McGurk, the Director of Intelligence, the Director of the FBI, the Secretary of Homeland Security, and the Attorney General have all stated publicly that the Islamic State of Iraq and Syria, or ISIS or ISIL, whichever one you want to call it, pose a direct threat to the United States. Do you agree?

Mr. MCGURK. Yes.

Senator MCCAIN. You do agree. Well, would you agree that Iraq and Syria are now effectively one conflict, that we cannot address ISIS in Iraq without also addressing it in Syria, and vice versa, particularly with reports that we see, published reports of equipment that was captured in Iraq now showing up in Syria?

Mr. MCGURK. I think it is one theater. It is the Tigris and Euphrates Valley theater, yes.

Senator MCCAIN. So you do believe that this caliphate, the richest and largest base of terrorism that I know of, is both Iraq and Syria, this enclave?

Mr. MCGURK. That is exactly what it is trying to do. It is trying to establish that.

Senator MCCAIN. Have they achieved it pretty well so far?

Mr. McGURK. Since June, the Iraq-Syria border has more or less collapsed.

Senator McCAIN. So that means really then, if we are going to take action in Iraq we should also take action in Syria; would you agree?

Mr. McGURK. Again, these are all options that are being looked at, Senator.

Senator McCAIN. I am just wondering if you would agree with that. I am not asking whether you are examining options or not.

Mr. McGURK. I think, Senator, as I mentioned, in order to really get at this network and learning from the past with Al Qaeda in Iraq, we have to squeeze the entire network. That is the foreign fighter flow, that is denying safe haven in Syria, and helping the Iraqis control their sovereign territory.

Senator McCAIN. So if we did initiate an air-to-ground campaign without including Syria, they would have a sanctuary in Syria. Would you agree with that?

Mr. McGURK. One of the reasons—and again, I would defer to my colleague Elissa—but we are focused on training the moderate opposition, to have a force that is able to deny safe haven and deny space to the ISL networks in Syria.

Senator McCAIN. Well, probably so. But the Secretary of Defense and the Chairman of the Joint Chiefs of Staff have both stated publicly that the Iraqi Security Forces are not capable of regaining the territory they have lost to ISIS on their own without external assistance. Do you agree with the Secretary of Defense and the Chairman of the Joint Chiefs?

Mr. McGURK. The Iraqi Security Forces have moved a little bit out of—we had the snowballing effect——

Senator McCAIN. I am again asking if you agree or disagree with the Secretary of Defense and the Chairman of the Joint Chiefs, who both stated publicly that the Iraq Security Forces are not capable of regaining the territory they have lost to ISIS on their own without external assistance. Do you agree or disagree?

Mr. McGURK. They cannot conduct combined arms-type operations, which is what it would take, without some enabling support.

Senator McCAIN. So since we all rule out boots on the ground, that might mean use of air power as a way of assisting them. Would you agree with that?

Mr. McGURK. Senator, all of these options and potential options for the President are being looked at and, as Elissa said, we are not going to crowd the decision space.

Senator McCAIN. How long have we been ''looking at'' them now, Mr. McGurk?

Mr. McGURK. Well——

Ms. SLOTKIN. Sir, the assessments came in last week.

Senator McCAIN. So the assessments came in last week. How long have we been assessing?

Ms. SLOTKIN. I think we assessed for two solid weeks.

Senator McCAIN. Oh, I think it has been longer than that since the collapse of the Iraqi military, Ms. Slotkin.

Ms. SLOTKIN. I think the President made his announcement on June 19 and then he instructed that assessors go to Baghdad. They flew there and began their assessments immediately.

Senator MCCAIN. I see. And so far we have launched no air strikes in any part of Iraq, right?

Ms. SLOTKIN. That is correct.

Senator MCCAIN. And you stated before that we did not have sufficient information to know which targets to hit, is that correct?

Ms. SLOTKIN. I think we have radically improved our intelligence picture.

Senator MCCAIN. But at the time in your view we did not have sufficient information capability in order to launch air strikes?

Ms. SLOTKIN. I think that, given our extremely deliberate process about launching any air strike, we would—

Senator MCCAIN. You know, it is interesting. I asked do you think at that time we did not have sufficient information to launch air strikes against ISIS.

Ms. SLOTKIN. I think, given the standards the United States has for dropping ordnance, no, we did not have the intelligence we would ever want at that time.

Senator MCCAIN. I find that interesting because none of the military that I have talked to that served there and even those who flew there—they are absolutely convinced, as I am, that when you have convoys moving across the desert in open terrain you can identify them and strike them. We know that they were operating out of bases in Syria, out in the open in the desert. So those of us who have some military experience in the efficacy of air power, we heartily disagree. And that is not just me. It comes from military leaders who served there.

Mr. McGurk, published media reports indicate that the Islamic State has an estimated 10,000 foreign fighters, 7,000 in Syria and 3,000 in Iraq. Does that sound right?

Mr. McGURK. These estimates are very difficult to discern, but that is an estimate that we routinely see, yes.

Senator MCCAIN. And of those foreign fighters, many of them are from European countries, right?

Mr. McGURK. Yes.

Senator MCCAIN. Who when returning to their countries do not require a visa to come to this country, which is why, as I say, the Director of National Intelligence, the Director of the FBI, and the Secretary of Homeland Security and the Attorney General have all stated that this poses a direct threat to the United States of America.

In light of that, do you think we are—so far, that we have had a proportionate response to that threat?

Mr. McGURK. I just want to say on the direct threat, if that is a direct quote from them, I obviously defer to them on the quote. One thing that we have done, I want to—in your questioning of Ms. Slotkin. When this crisis started the Iraqis had zero Hellfire missiles in their arsenal. We have delivered to them, since this crisis began in June, hundreds of Hellfire missiles. And with our new intelligence, with the joint operations center, the Iraqis have deployed those missiles with precision and accuracy. It has made a difference, and I would be happy to follow up to——

Senator MCCAIN. Excuse me. What difference has it made?

Mr. MCGURK. Well, it blunted some of——

Senator MCCAIN. Certainly not in the areas of Iraq that the ISIS has been able to gain control over.

Mr. MCGURK. It began to blunt some of the momentum. Seriously, we certainly have a lot more——

Senator MCCAIN. You did not really believe that they could take Baghdad, did you? No one in their right mind would.

Mr. MCGURK. In the initial days of this crisis, there was a very deep concern that Iraqi Security Forces could, in the approaches to Baghdad, substantially weaken and that was a real concern of ours.

Senator MCCAIN. Well, there might have been on your part, but it certainly was not on those of us who understand Iraq and population and Shia and Sunni.

Well, Mr. Chairman, I have overstayed my time. I thank you, but I really agree with you, Ms. Slotkin, when you said you cannot fight something with nothing. You are exactly right.

The CHAIRMAN. Senator Kaine.

Senator KAINE. Thank you, Mr. Chairman.

Odds and ends because most of my questions have been asked already by my colleagues. But give me the status on the safety of the American Embassy in Baghdad and our consuls in Iraq?

Mr. MCGURK. Senator, thank you. It is our foremost priority. It is something we watch every day very closely. That is why we have rebalanced our security apparatus at the Embassy. We have brought in substantial Department of Defense capabilities into the Embassy and into the airport. Our Assistant Secretary for Diplomatic Security was there last week, and we feel very confident about the protection of our people. But it is something that we watch literally every second of every day.

Our knowledge and our understanding of the defense of Baghdad, in particular, is night and day different from where it was just 6 weeks ago.

Senator KAINE. Because of the deployment of the advisers, as you were discussing?

Mr. MCGURK. Yes.

Senator KAINE. Let me ask about this, the Iranian influence in Iraq. Beyond political influence, how about Iranian expenditures in Iraq, whether it is to back up the military or provide training and assistance? What is Iran doing in Iraq right now that is costing them money?

Mr. MCGURK. I do not have a figure on the expenditures. All I can say is that the Iraqis again, they want the United States to be the backbone of their military force, and that is why they have looked to the FMS program to be that backbone. Where we have developed relationships with Iraqi military officers, even in times of extreme crisis, it has proven essential. An example in my testimony is that when we had to get about 500 contractors out of Bilad, it was the Iraqi Air Force, even despite the extreme crisis they were dealing with, that flew their own C–130s with their own pilots to get our people out. That is the kind of relationship that we need to continue to invest in.

Senator KAINE. I just want to, because I am going in a particular direction with this. You do not have an expenditure figure on what Iran is spending in Iraq, but are they likely spending significant resources or is the influence just more kind of more on the political and relationship side?

Mr. MCGURK. They are expending resources. They were particularly concerned about the defense of Samarra, where the Golden Dome Al-Askari Mosque is. And in the early weeks of the crisis, they did invest resources to try to protect that area of Samarra.

Senator KAINE. The reason I am asking this question is separately we are having this intense discussion about the Iranian nuclear negotiation and what is the effect of the sanctions on Iran and to what extent any sanctions relief is giving them breathing room. And we are being told from many quarters that the Iranian economy is still suffering very greatly. They seem to be pretty deeply in, in terms of expenditures in Syria and they seem to be pretty deeply in in terms of expenditures in Iraq, and that makes me think either they are incredibly stretched or maybe their economy and resources are a little bit stronger than some of the reports to us suggest. And that is relevant in terms of the negotiations that are underway with respect to the nuclear program. I will follow that up with others.

This is a question that you might not be able to answer on the record, and if so I will submit it—or in public—I will submit it for the record. What are the efforts under way by the United States to disrupt ISIL financing?

Ms. SLOTKIN. Sir, I think we should take it off the record if you do not mind, just in a classified session. I would be happy to provide that to you.

Senator KAINE. We have had testimony in these hearings before about some kinds of financing that I think can be talked about publicly. They do extortion, they do kidnapping. They go to merchants and say: Pay us X. That has been discussed publicly. But there has also been reports about others who are funding ISIL operations, often others—maybe not the government, but people who are connected with governments that are allies of ours. And I would like to know in a classified setting—and we will submit a written question—what are we doing to disrupt ISIL financing?

The persecution of the Christian minority in Iraq, like the persecution of any religious minority, is of significance. Could you talk about your recent discussions on the persecution of Christians when you were in Baghdad, Mr. McGurk?

Mr. MCGURK. Thank you, Senator. I went to the home of the Chaldean patriarch, Archbishop Sako in Mansour in Baghdad, to discuss this directly with him, and then also in Erbil with Bishop Warda. It is an extremely serious situation. What is so inspiring when you visit them is that Archbishop Sako, shortly before I saw him, had just had a service with about 500 worshippers from across the city of Baghdad in his church. This past Sunday he had a service in which Muslims and Christians came together in his church to say: ''We are all Christians, we all stand for the Christians, we are all Iraqis, these are all our people, to stand against ISIL.''

Bishop Warda in Erbil is focused on the refugees that have left Mosul and he has asked us for some specific help with the Kurdish

Regional Government to ensure they have the protection they need, and that is something that we followed up with President Barzani immediately after that meeting, to ensure that they do have that protection. And it is something we are working on every day.

But it is a very serious situation, and it reveals what is happening to the Christians in Mosul, it reveals what ISIL is all about and why it is such a threat to the region and to us.

Senator KAINE. Again, we should feel deeply—since the United States stands so strongly for religious liberty, we should feel deeply about the persecution of any religious minority. Mass has been said in Mosul for more than 1,800 years, but for the first time that has been broken. Weekly mass is not being celebrated there. That is a pretty significant thing.

I have been critical of us, the Senate, for slowness in ambassadorial approvals, but I will just put one on the administration. You also have got to get us names. And I will just say this for the record: The Ambassador at Large for International Religious Freedom post has been vacant since October 2013. The White House has not sent us a name, at a time in the world, whether it might be Christians or Ahmadiyya Muslims or Jews in some nations that are suffering because of the persecution of religious minorities. And sadly, while the United States is an example of religious diversity, we see these persecution of minorities probably on the increase in the world.

It is a core value of ours. We have such a good story to tell. That should not be a position that is vacant. I encourage the administration to send us a nominee promptly.

With that, Mr. Chair, I have no more questions.

The CHAIRMAN. Senator Markey.

Senator MARKEY. Thank you, Mr. Chairman, very much.

I would like to focus on the role of energy resources in the conflict with ISIS and in the Iraqi leadership's struggle to maintain a workable political system. ISIS has taken over the oil fields near Mosul and Tikrit and continues to have its sights set on the Baiji oil refinery, Iraq's largest. The group continues to control oil fields in northeast Syria. Smuggling this oil into the black market has reportedly brought ISIS millions in revenues, perhaps a million dollars a day it is being reported.

With the group's ambition to take on the trappings of an actual state, how does capturing energy resources and infrastructure fit into their broader strategy?

Mr. McGURK. They need the resources to survive. One reason they are coming with everything they have at the Baiji refinery is because they need the energy resources that are stored in those tanks in order to keep Mosul running. The Baiji refinery battle has now been going on for a month. There is a unit of Iraq's Counterterrorism Service Forces there, people that we know and that we have trained, who have been fighting incredibly heroically.

ISIL has sent waves of car bombs and suicide bombers at the refinery. So far the Iraqis continue to hold it, although it is a very desperate struggle. But strategically it desperately needs these resources to, as you said, be able to build——

Senator MARKEY. What further steps need to be taken in order to protect against ISIS taking over the Baiji refinery? That is a critical moment in the whole struggle if they are successful in doing that, the largest single refinery in the country. What can be done, what needs to be done, in order to prevent that from happening?

Mr. McGURK. Well, in fact, as I mentioned briefly in the answer to some of Senator McCain's questions, when we did get the Hellfire missiles into the country, one of the first places they were deployed was around the Baiji refinery, to begin to clear out some of the attacking ISL fighters. So that is one example.

As we continue to assess the situation in Iraq, we have identified particular strategic sites that we are concerned about and that we want to make sure the Iraqis have whatever capabilities they might need to be able to defend them.

Senator MARKEY. Let me move on to the Kurdish Regional Government in the north. The Kurds are sitting on an estimated reserve of 45 billion barrels of oil and have now captured the oil fields around Kirkuk as well. They appear to be more and more intent on selling their own oil abroad without coordinating those exports through the central authorities in Baghdad, and Baghdad seems unwilling to equitably distribute the country's oil resources.

How can we help the Iraqi Government to better manage its energy resources and preserve a federal system that works for all Iraqis? Right now that seems to be collapsing and the collapse is over the oil revenue issue. How can we play a bigger role?

Mr. McGURK. Well, this is something where we can play a direct role, and it is one reason we had to get through the election and start to get a new government formed, so we can get some traction on this issue. Again, the numbers really tell the story. The Kurds need about $14 billion in order to really sustain themselves. Their own exports right now, they approach a little less than half of that probably. That will change over the future.

The budget that is pending in Baghdad, that is before the Parliament, is a $140 billion budget. The Kurdish share of that would be a little more than $17 billion. So the numbers really tell the story and the numbers give the trade space for how we can work out a deal.

Again, there are new realities on the ground that we have to deal with, but it is in the interest of all Iraqis to export as much oil as possible under a revenue-sharing framework, particularly for the Sunni areas of Iraq, which do not have any of these natural resources. And that is the type of compact that I think a new Government, and particularly the new Parliament, which has proven to be very effective—and they just set up a committee to try to resolve this—can get some traction on.

But we have to be actively engaged because we are the one neutral broker between all of these parties, and without us they will not get there.

Senator MARKEY. Again, oil is always at the core of this? Cherchez the oil, that is pretty much what it is all about. That is why the British wanted the country constructed the way it was. They wanted those oil resources, especially up in the north, added, even though it was going to cause longer term instability. But that is what they were fighting for. That is what they were demanding in those negotiations 80 years ago, 90 years ago. And we are still living with the consequences of those decisions.

Let me just move on then and ask, what is the current relationship between ISIS and al-Qaeda? What has happened to that relationship in the course of especially the last 3 or 4 months?

Mr. McGURK. Well, it is my understanding Al Qaeda in Iraq, of course, was Zarqawi's group and it had pledged adherence and allegiance to al-Qaeda central in Pakistan and Afghanistan. When it moved into Syria it split into two groups, the al-Nusra Front and what has become the Islamic State of Iraq and the Levant.

The Islamic State of Iraq and the Levant had ambitions across borders between Iraq and Syria and that is something that senior al-Qaeda leaders such as Zawahiri did not agree with and he issued an edict saying: I do not agree with that; you should all work as one, or ISIS should work in Iraq and Nusra works in Syria. And Abu Bakr al-Baghdadi said: I do not agree with you on that, so I am going to go my own way. And that is what led to the split.

But ISIL is proving to be in many ways even more effective in terms of organizing and developing a state structure than even core al-Qaeda, and that is why it is more than just a terrorist organization. It certainly does not have the global reach in terms of terrorist capacity as core al-Qaeda, but it has the sophistication to develop what is really becoming a state-like sanctuary for a global jihadist movement. And Baghdadi has now made clear he is reaching for the mantle of the global jihad, and trying to recruit those who share that ideology from all around the world.

Senator MARKEY. So what does that competitive dynamic between the leaders of both groups ultimately potentially lead to?

Mr. McGURK. Well, the risk is that, in terms of that competition, they will look to external attack plotting in order to do spectacular type attacks to further draw worldwide recruits. That is the risk.

Senator MARKEY. I think you have already answered the questions about recruiting. Let me just ask a final question and that is about Iraqi Forces' capacity to defend their own civilians. Could you just give us a brief summary of where you believe they are right now in accomplishing that goal?

Mr. McGURK. Well, one reason I said in my testimony, we have a counterterrorism challenge; Iraq has a counterinsurgency challenge. A counterinsurgency challenge means they have to be able to control their own population and that is why they have to recruit locally and work with tribes that control local areas.

Right now that has really broken apart, and it has broken apart for a number of reasons, but primarily the force that ISIL is able to bring to bear in some of the Sunni areas of Iraq. They go after anybody that disagrees with them. They have a bit of an alliance with the Naqshbandi and the Baath Party networks, but even that is starting to fray. So this is why we have to work with the Iraqis to be able to protect their population against the most violent groups and then work on the political compact to make sure that all areas of Iraq have the resources they need to sustain themselves.

Senator MARKEY. Again, I want to commend you for your focus on diplomacy. I agree with Ryan Crocker that it is not too late for diplomacy, but we just have to be intervening in a very, very aggressive way to make sure that diplomacy is truly given a chance to be successful.

Thank you so much. Thank you, Mr. Chairman.

Senator KAINE [presiding]. Thank you, Senator Markey.

Thank you to the witnesses. We will leave the record open until 5 o'clock tomorrow for the submission of questions. We would appreciate your prompt responses. Thank you for your testimony.

We have a superb second panel and I would ask them to come forward now. As we are setting up for the second panel, let me just let all know who we will have. We are fortunate to have: former U.S. Ambassador to Iraq Jim Jeffrey, who is currently at the Washington Institute on Near East Policy; Lieutenant General Michael Barbero, who served nearly 4 years in Iraq over three tours. General Barbero has traveled to Iraq six times in the last year while serving as the Director of the Joint Improvised Explosive Device Defeat Organization. Finally, no stranger to the committee, Dr. Ken Pollack, who has been a respected voice on Iraq and the gulf from his time in the CIA, the National Security Council, now at the Brookings Institute.

This is a superb panel and we are glad to have everyone here. Let me just, to the panel and the audience, I apologize. The challenge of being on the second panel, everybody comes and has a million questions and then about lunch time races off, and it is unfortunate that all will not be here to hear you live. But we really do appreciate you being here today because your experiences each give you something very important to add.

Your written statements, which were very strong, will be obviously included in the entire record. We would like to ask each to take about 5 minutes to summarize, and I will have you speak in the order I introduced you, beginning with Ambassador Jeffrey and moving from my right to left. Ambassador Jeffrey, welcome.

STATEMENT OF HON. JAMES F. JEFFREY, PHILIP SOLONDZ DISTINGUISHED VISITING FELLOW, THE WASHINGTON INSTITUTE FOR NEAR EAST POLICY, WASHINGTON, DC

Ambassador JEFFREY. Thank you very much, Mr. Acting Chairman.

To follow up on what we heard this morning, the establishment of the Islamic State by the ISIL in Iraq and in parts of Syria is changing the geostrategy of the entire Middle East and represents a dramatic setback to United States policy and interests and requires an immediate response from Washington. The situation is complicated by the fact that in the fix we are presently in in the Middle East we have not one, but two, hegemonic radical forces in the region, from Gaza to Iran, that are trying to upset the established order throughout the Middle East, and we have to deal with all of them in a comprehensive way.

The President's plan to support a unified Iraq in this crisis as laid out on June 19 is reasonable, but over a month has gone by, as we discussed earlier today, and very little has happened. In government formation, we have had two important but secondary steps, the selection of the Speaker and the selection of a President from the Kurdish community. Those are important, but those are basically the preliminaries. The key issue is the selection of a Prime Minister and a new Government.

Meanwhile, on the ground, while the initial ISIL drive on Baghdad and on the strategic areas has been slowed, we are seeing new offensive capabilities by that organization. The Institute for the Study of War came out yesterday with a survey of attacks, both suicide and what we call VBIEDs, vehicle bombs, inside Baghdad and efforts to try to cut off the city. Senator McCain was right that you cannot take Baghdad, but, as almost happened to us with over 100,000 troops in 2004, you can isolate the city, and they seem to be trying to do that.

Meanwhile, they are pushing against the Kurds all along the 400-mile front from the Iranian border to north of Mosul and they are trying to seize strategic infrastructure. Baiji we talked about, but also the Haditha Dam west of Ramadi and the Mosul Dam on the Tigris River to the northeast of Mosul. These are extraor- dinarily important infrastructure targets for them. So we do have an offensive threat from that organization.

The President's plan is based upon, above all, a new inclusive government. As I said, while we have done the preliminaries with the Speaker and with the President, we have not gotten to the key issue of who is going to govern the country, because the Prime Minister essentially governs the country. In my view the inclusive government that the President has correctly said is a prerequisite to any real action cannot be a government headed by Prime Minister Maliki. He simply has not shown the ability to bring in the Kurdish and the Sunni communities, and that is needed right now because there is a huge division of both trust and geographic division in the country today.

We also need to encourage the Kurds, as Mr. McGurk described in some detail, to remain within the republic and try to regain trust among the Sunnis. Again, I see this as only possible if we have a new Prime Minister and a new Government.

Simultaneously, I think that, while the President is right that we cannot do a major campaign until we get an inclusive government that can provide essentially people on the ground, local forces, we need to do limited strikes. General Dempsey talked about some of the possibilities, going after key leaders and strategic infrastructure. We need to do a little bit of that now, in part to encourage everybody to come together.

Mr. McGurk talked about the Sunni tribes that are trying to fight ISIS, but they are outgunned. Helping them would not be undercutting a new government. The Kurds are fighting all along the front and they need help. We heard about some of these highly trained, effective Iraqi units that are still in the fight, particularly north of Baghdad. They could benefit from help, too.

We are striking al-Qaeda right now in Pakistan, Yemen, and with direct actions at times in Somalia and Libya. I see no reason why we could not—if we have the targets and we are getting the data now—start doing some strikes both in Iraq and in Syria.

Meanwhile, we have to be ready, though. If this does not work out, if the Iranians remain influential in Baghdad, if Mr. Maliki remains in power, if the groups cannot come together, we have to start thinking about how are we going to deal if we do have three separate entities—a Kurdistan that will be a magnet for Kurds throughout the region; effectively a Taliban-like Islamic State in the middle of the Levant; and a rump Iraq that is ever more under the control or under the influence of Iran. That is a huge new problem for us if we do not act very, very quickly.

So my bottom line here today, sir, is that we need to act as quickly as we can.

[The prepared statement of Ambassador Jeffrey follows:]

PREPARED STATEMENT OF AMBASSADOR JAMES FRANKLIN JEFFREY

The establishment of the Islamic State (IS) by the Al Qaeda in Iraq offshoot group Islamic State of Iraq and Levant (ISIL) changes the geostrategy of the entire Middle East, represents a dramatic setback to U.S. policy and interests, and requires an immediate response from Washington. The creation of an extremist quasi-state, analogous to Afghanistan under the Taliban, carries the risk of further escalation including a regional Sunni-Shia conflict, and an irreparable loss in U.S. influence. But the rise of the ISIL first in Syria and now in Iraq reflects in part the nefarious effort by Iran to exploit sectarian divides to achieve regional hegemony. The U.S. Government must counter both the IS threat and Iran's quest for domination, bearing in mind that Iran is not our ally in the campaign against al-Qaeda terror. Above all, the U.S. must recognize that we are in a full blown crisis that requires action, even if politically risky.

THE SITUATION

The rise of the IS, with control over up to 5 million people and massive military equipment and funding, in close proximity to some of the largest oil fields in the world, and bordering our NATO ally Turkey and security partners Jordan, Saudi Arabia, and Kuwait, threatens three of the four vital interests President Obama laid out in his U.N. General Assembly speech last September: threats to or allies and partners, rise of terrorist organizations, and threats to international flow of oil. The situation if it deteriorates further will likely threaten the fourth, development of weapons of mass destruction, as Iran, in part influenced by events in Iraq, is balking at a compromise outcome of the nuclear negotiations with the P5+1.

A traditional approach to IS based on maintaining a unified Iraq, while building up the Iraqi Government, the Kurdistan Regional Government (KRG), and Sunni elements willing to resist ISIL, is the best option, but it may not long be attainable. Despite the election of a moderate Sunni Arab speaker of the Iraqi Parliament 2 weeks ago, there is no certainty that Iraqi political leaders and Parliament can overcome their deep divisions to create an inclusive new government as rightly demanded by the U.S. Government. For starters, any such government must not be headed by PM Maliki. He has lost the trust of many of his citizens, including a great many Shia Arabs, yet is still trying to hold on to power. In this uncertain situation, while pushing the traditional approach, we must simultaneously prepare to deal with an Iraq semipermanently split into three separate political entities, and to shape our approach to the Sunni Arab, Shia Arab, and Kurdish populations and to the central government on that basis.

But with either the traditional or this possible new approach, American military force under certain circumstances must be used against ISIL, for political as well as military and counterterrorism reasons, and everyone in the U.S. must understand that we are in an emergency. The costs of doing little or nothing now are greater than the risks of most actions short of committing ground troops.

CONTINUING OUR TRADITIONAL POLICIES

The President's course of action outlined in his Iraq speech of June 19 is reasonable: protect our Baghdad Embassy, strengthen our intelligence and military presence in and around Iraq, increase assistance to the Iraqi military, and press the Iraqi political system to support a new, inclusive government which can reach out to estranged Sunni Arabs and Kurds and maintain the country's unity; only then with our help can it begin to retake areas held by the IS. This approach, reflecting our traditional policy toward a united Iraq, remains the best option, but over a month has passed since the President laid out this policy, and we have had little followthrough beyond better intelligence collection and on-the-ground coordination. That is important but not sufficient, and now it is not clear if we still have time to carry out this course of action.

To maximize the chances of a unified, inclusive Iraq to which we can provide significant new military assistance including air strikes, the following needs to occur in the days ahead:

—The Iraqi Parliament, charged with forming a new government after the March elections, must decide on a Prime Minister other than Nuri al-Maliki. Few Sunni Arabs or Kurds will believe that any Iraqi Government is inclusive and would consider their interests if Maliki remains its leader. Promises to be inclusive and nonsectarian are cheap in Baghdad, but followthrough usually lacking. The most convincing proof that politicians have gotten the "be inclusive" message is for Maliki to step down, or be forced out by his own and other Shia parties. Removing Maliki is not a direct U.S. responsibility, and too obvious a U.S. push would be counterproductive. But we must make clear to all parties that decisive American support can only come with an inclusive government and buy-in by all major sectarian groups, and that this is not possible with Maliki.

—The Kurdistan Regional Government must forgo its threats of independence in return for a government that will consider their interests. Finding a replacement for Maliki is necessary but not sufficient to win the Kurds back. This will require compromises on Kurdish oil exports building on a December 2013 agreement on calculating oil shares, and renewed payment by Baghdad of the Kurds' 17 percent share of southern oil exports. The Kurds in turn will have to share their oil proceeds 17–83 percent between themselves and Baghdad, which they claim they will do, and exercise restraint on the status of the Kirkuk field, which they have not committed to do. The U.S. should push for such a solution by pressing both the Kurds directly and through their informal partner, Turkey, to engage fully the central government. Kurdish thirst for independence is understandable, but under current circumstances it is a recipe for reduced hydrocarbons income to the KRG for years, turmoil with the rest of Iraq, and resistance from regional states. It is thus a last option, not a first choice.

—Any new Iraqi leadership must also win over Sunni Arabs. A commitment to provide significant oil revenue earnings to individual provinces (as has occurred already with the KRG, Basra, Najaf, and Kirkuk provinces) would provide concrete evidence of outreach to Sunni Arabs, and promote Iraq's federal system and probably government efficiency at the same time.

—A new Defense Minister from the Sunni Arab community, with very strong commitments by all parties to lead the military in fact, must be quickly selected once a new Prime Minister is chosen.

—As noted above, the U.S. cannot consider decisive U.S. strikes until Iraq has an inclusive government which will resonate with many Sunni Arabs. The administration, in line with the President's June 19 remarks, clearly is using possible U.S. military action as leverage to ensure such a government. That makes sense, but it is not incompatible with limited U.S. strikes for objectives similar to those General Dempsey spelled out recently—to protect population centers and strategic infrastructure and target ISIL leadership. Limited strikes now for such strategic purposes make sense. Any day is a good day to strike an al-Qaeda offshoot as dangerous as this one. People to whom we have given commitments, not just the Iraqi military but many Sunni Arabs and the Kurdish Peshmerga, are today locked in combat with ISIL, and need help. Especially given the recent record of American reticence in using force, limited strikes avoiding civilian areas now would increase, not decrease, our political leverage.

—The U.S. should rapidly deploy its $500 million committed to train and equip the Syrian opposition. The U.S. should also strike against IS in Syria.

—Once these steps have been taken, the U.S. can plan with the Iraqi Government, KRG, friendly Iraqi Sunni Arabs, and regional partners, to retake those Iraqi areas now held by the IS. Such a counterinsurgency plan would include aggressive U.S. training, equipping, and coordinating, intelligence, and air strikes, along with action by Sunni Arabs willing with our help to take on IS.

A DIVIDED IRAQ?

While the above is aligned with administration policy, and in theory offers the best way forward, it may be too late to implement it, as the divisions between the various Iraqi groups deepen, sectarian slaughter especially of Sunni Arabs in and around Baghdad continues, and the KRG moves toward virtual independence, all with Maliki still in office.

Were this to occur, the U.S. must deal with three separate entities, all posing significant problems for American interests: an IS threatening us, as well as our allies and partners, and a magnet for jihadist supporters world-wide; a KRG moving toward a de jure breakup with Baghdad, raising the specter of a Near East-wide quest for a Kurdish nation-state which would undermine existing borders; and a rump Iraq, dominated by Shia religious parties heavily influenced by Iran, and controlling what the International Energy Agency believes could well be exports of 6 million barrels of oil by 2020—almost two-thirds of Saudi Arabia's exports.

If this materializes, the U.S. must de facto abandon a policy prioritizing Iraqi unity. The first priority rather should be to deter and if necessary defeat IS attacks on Jordan, the KRG, and other partners and allies. Policy coordination with Turkey, Jordan, Israel, the KRG, and the Gulf States, important in any scenario, would be vital in this one, first as a shield for vulnerable states and groups, and then as a platform to destroy the IS. Such coordination would require much greater U.S. support for the Syrian opposition, caution with outreach to the KRG, whose independent status is anathema not just to Baghdad but to Arab States, and continued containment of Iran. It would also require U.S. strikes against IS in both Iraq and Syria.

In such a scenario, U.S. policy toward Baghdad would inevitably evolve. To the extent the rump central government is willing to cooperate with us, and avoid provoking the Kurds and the Sunni Arabs further, then limited U.S. military support under the FMS program should continue, as should direct U.S. military action against IS attacks against Shia population centers. This policy will require constant review depending upon how influential Iran is in Baghdad, and how Baghdad treats its Kurdish and Sunni Arab citizens. The experience with Maliki in the past several months gives little hope that such treatment would improve as long as he remains in power.

IRAN

The U.S. can talk with Iran about Iraq, emphasizing common interests such as unity of the state and the fight against IS, but we do not share common goals. In the fix we are presently in we have not one but two hegemonic Islamic radical forces intent on overthrowing the prevailing nation-state order in the region—al-Qaeda especially IS, and the Islamic Republic of Iran. And our allies in the common struggle for stability—Turkey, Israel, and the Sunni Arab States—see Iran as at least an equal threat to their survival as al-Qaeda.

But we also must do everything possible to avoid a regional "Sunni versus Shia" conflict. Such a conflict would tear the region apart, and any U.S. involvement would have us violating our "we fight for liberal principles, not sectarian interests" policy that we have been able to maintain in the region and elsewhere, such as in the Balkans.

Senator KAINE. Thank you, Ambassador Jeffrey.
General Barbero.

STATEMENT OF MICHAEL D. BARBERO, LIEUTENANT GENERAL, U.S. ARMY [RETIRED], WASHINGTON, DC

General BARBERO. Thank you, Mr. Ranking Chairman, Ranking Member Corker. Thank you for the opportunity to discuss the situation in Iraq and some options moving forward. I will focus my comments on the security sector, the Iraqi Security Forces, and some recommendations therein.

But first I would like to start with several observations on the current situation. Time accrues to the benefit of ISIS. While we assess, they maintain the momentum, they grow stronger, and their hold on the population intensifies. ISIS has established control across a contiguous area in both Syria and Iraq and, as we discussed in the previous panel, it must be considered as an Iraq-Syria front.

ISIS poses a formidable regional threat. What is most frightening is as they swept into Iraq they continued their expansion into Syria. They did not have to thin the lines to do that.

The Iraqi Security Forces have regrouped. However, these forces have serious fundamental flaws and will require significant assistance to be able to undertake counteroffensives to dislodge and roll back ISIS control.

Finally, ISIS is an existential threat to both Baghdad and the Kurds. The Kurds have a 1,000-plus kilometer border or front with ISIS and they are largely on their own.

Chairman Menendez asked at the outset, what is required to turn back the tide of ISIS? Well, it is clearly the Iraqi Security Forces. But my estimation is in their present state they cannot successfully meet this ISIS threat, let alone mount a major and effective counteroffensive without significant assistance. The capabilities necessary to counter ISIS do not exist today in Iraq and they will not likely materialize on their own.

I am not talking in the future about ground combat forces from the United States. I am talking about advising and assisting in certain key areas. Let me cover those. The first is intelligence, and we have started that, developing tactical intelligence and targetable, actionable intelligence on the ground. We have started that. Now we need to turn that into action.

But the second intelligence component is the ISIS network in Iraq, Syria, and their regional supporters must be a national collection and analysis priority for our entire intelligence community.

Second, we should establish a training program for the ISF to develop sufficient combined arms capability in order to effectively conduct offensive operations to dislodge ISIS from the areas they now control. The ISF has been largely a checkpoint army. Since 2011 their operations have been defensive in nature, static in disposition, and disjointed in execution. They need training.

Third, they need assistance in establishing an effective wartime sustainment structure and process. Their existing one is a peacetime system and they have experienced significant decline in equipment readiness over the years, and this will be a daunting process, but it can be done.

Fourth, they require changes to their command and control network. As we know, the system now in place is one put in by Prime Minister Maliki of area commands directly reporting to him. As we have seen, there needs to be changes in commanders and changes to develop an effective combat command and control capability.

Fifth, the ISF continues to need weapons and equipment. We have done some good work to rush some equipment there, but we need to do more. Just this week Iraq's Ambassador to the United States lamented the slow pace of our support when compared to the rapid support from Iran and Russia. We should quickly approve, ship, and enable material support to Iraq.

Sixth, we should support the ISF with air strikes in order to degrade ISIS capabilities. But let me be clear. You cannot air strike or drone strike your way out of this. Air strikes must be part of a cohesive and coherent counteroffensive in order to attack ISIS.

Seventh, we should support the Kurds and enable them to defend against this existential threat from ISIS. The Pesh Merga are an effective, determined, well-led force. However, they are lightly armed and underequipped. They are stretched very thin, and when ISIS turns on them they will be outgunned and overmatched.

Now, there is a complex relationship between Baghdad and Erbil. I understand that. But why would we not, from a purely tactical and security perspective, why would we not rapidly enable the Kurds to defend northern Iraq from ISIS, prevent the oil-rich north from falling into ISIS hands, and force ISIS to fight on two fronts in Iraq?

Finally, this all depends on two things: a willing partner in Baghdad that is willing to accept these changes and to help develop an effective ISF; and second, as we all discussed, there must be a political climate where the Sunni and Kurds feel accommodation for them and they could join in a unified military action.

In conclusion, it is an existential threat to Iraq. The longer we wait to decide on our response to Iraq's request for support, the stronger they become. Finally, if the prevention of an ISIS-controlled Iraq is in the national interest of the United States, then we should act to aid and enable Iraq and the Kurds to defeat this threat as quickly as possible.

Thank you, Mr. Chairman, for the opportunity.

[The prepared statement of General Barbero follows:]

STATEMENT OF LTG MICHAEL D. BARBERO

Chairman Menendez, Ranking Member Corker, and distinguished members of the committee, thank you for inviting me to appear before you today to discuss the situation in Iraq and options for U.S. policy there.

One year ago I retired following 38 years of Active Duty, during which I spent three tours of duty in Iraq, spending a total of 46 months in Iraq. Since my retirement, over the past year, I have been back to Iraq—in Erbil, Baghdad, and Basra—6 times, maintaining close contact with many Shia, Sunni, and Kurdish leaders. So, Iraq and its future is a subject of great personal importance to me.

I am especially honored to appear with these two distinguished fellow panelists who are respected experts on the subject of today's hearing. And given the broad and deep expertise of Ambassador Jeffrey and Doctor Pollack, I will focus my remarks on the security sector—the current security situation and recommendations on options for our security policy moving forward.

I would like begin with several overall observations on the current security situation; followed by an assessment of the ISIS threat, and finishing with recommendations on assistance to Iraq's security needs.

OBSERVATIONS ON THE CURRENT SITUATION

- Time accrues to the benefit of ISIS; while we "assess" they maintain the momentum, they grow stronger, and their hold on the population intensifies. ISIS continues to exert its control, consolidate gains, and build a state.
- ISIS has established control across a contiguous area in both Syria and Iraq and we must realize it is the Iraq-Syria front, not just think in terms of Iraq.
- ISIS poses a formidable regional threat. As it executed its sweeping campaign in Iraq, ISIS simultaneously continued its campaign expansion in Eastern Syria and has the strategy and capabilities to continue the offensive.
- The Iraqi Security Forces have regrouped and stopped the ISIS advance. However these forces have serious, fundamental flaws and will require significant assistance to be able to undertake a counteroffensive to dislodge and roll back ISIS control.
- ISIS is an existential threat to both Baghdad and the Kurds. The Kurds have a 1,000+ KM border/front with ISIS and they are largely on their own. It is time to assist and enable the Kurds in their fight with ISIS.

Now, I would like to elaborate on these points and discuss the security situation in Iraq.

ISIS and the Syria-Iraq Front

ISIS seeks to create an Islamic Caliphate extending across Syria and Iraq by first destroying the existing state boundaries of Iraq and Syria and expanding the territory under their control. It is a mistake to consider ISIS actions in Iraq in isolation. Rather, ISIS must be viewed in the new reality that it has established control over major, contiguous areas of Syria and Iraq.

In Syria, following the declaration of a caliphate by ISIS leader Abu Bakr al-Baghdadi, a cascade of surrenders by rebel and tribal brigades in Syria's Deir ez-Zour province conferred large swaths of territorial control to ISIS. Beginning on July 2, these advances dramatically changed the balance of power within the province and provided ISIS the opportunity to achieve territorial continuity along the Euphrates River into Iraq's al-Anbar province. ISIS has successfully linked its territorial control between its ar-Raqqa stronghold and Deir ez-Zour City, solidifying an ISIS control zone that stretches from ar-Raqqa into Iraq's al-Anbar province. ISIS seized control of eight towns located northwest of Deir ez-Zour city from the al-Bosarya tribe on July 18. This advance comes as Jabhat al-Nusra (JN) and Ahrar al-Sham forces surrendered control of the towns of as-Shametia and Jabal Kabous to ISIS, abandoned their local headquarters and withdrawing from the province.

The surrender of a large number of local rebel and tribal brigades to ISIS in Syria's Deir ez-Zour province was a reflection and result of ISIS success in Iraq. Driven by apprehension in the wake of ISIS's success in Iraq, a number of local leaders sought to avoid an armed takeover by reinvigorated ISIS forces and agreed to a set of ISIS-imposed conditions for the peaceful surrender of rebel forces. These agreements allowed ISIS to quickly and efficiently assert full control over a large swath of territory whose armed takeover would have otherwise required a significant and costly ISIS ground offensive. Critically, further surrenders have occurred as ISIS began to consolidate. In addition to providing an additional windfall of weaponry, these surrenders have expanded ISIS's zones of control and sustained the current ISIS momentum within the province.

According to some reports ISIS now controls 35 percent of Syrian territory and the Syrian regime has been unable to meaningfully challenge the ISIS advance.

In Iraq, as evidence that actions in Syria and in Iraq are closely linked, ISIS completed its military operation to connect its line of communication between its strongholds in ar-Raqqa, Deir ez-Zour and Mosul, Iraq. For example, ISIS has extended its campaign against primarily Kurdish-protected areas by attacking in Sinjar. Sinjar, which has been quiet since Tal Afar fell, may become a more significant focus for ISIS.

In Baghdad, ISIS's Vehicle-Born Improvised Explosive Devices (VBIED) campaign is active again, relaunching its signature wave of VBIEDs attacks. Multiple, near-simultaneous attacks are the signature strategy that ISIS pursued as it gained strength in 2012 and 2013. In the first significant use of VBIEDs since a wave of attacks occurred on May 13, 2014, last Saturday on 19 July, multiple VBIEDs detonated in Baghdad's Shia neighborhoods. I believe these actions portend an ISIS campaign to attack Baghdad as part of its strategic campaign the secure Baghdad. Spectacular attacks in the form of VBIED and indirect fire attacks against Shia and Government targets in Baghdad, including Baghdad International Airport will be accompanied by ''conventional'' ground attacks to turn Baghdad into a war zone.

Across the Syria-Iraq front, ISIS possesses the momentum in all areas and will continue its operations to assert control over occupied territories, continue its assault in Iraq to secure its lines of communication and expand its control over strategic objectives.

Iraqi Security Forces

Iraqi Security Forces (ISF), in their present state, cannot successfully meet this ISIS threat, let alone mount a major and effective counteroffensive, without significant assistance. Preparing ISF for an effective counteroffensive operation requires extensive preparation; it cannot be thrown together in days or weeks. The capabilities necessary to counter ISIS do not exist today in Iraq and they will not likely materialize on their own anytime soon.

Let me be clear—I am not talking about a direct ground combat role for U.S. Forces. However, enabling the ISF to be successful against ISIS will require robust advising and enabling by American Forces, and this effort must be started immediately and executed simultaneously in several critical areas.

First, the decisive way to defeat an ISIS force is to attack its entire network: its leaders, financiers, suppliers and key operators, combat capabilities and front line fighters. However, generating targetable intelligence to attack ISIS requires a deep understanding of the network, which is only gained through a robust and effective intelligence effort over time. This intelligence support has two components. First, this requires an investment of personnel and technical intelligence capabilities in Iraq to develop an intelligence system that integrates all types of intelligence from all sources. The ISF need support in tactical intelligence collection, analysis and dissemination in order to understand the ISIS structure and develop targets. In the absence of this actionable intelligence, independent ground operations or isolated airstrikes, as we have seen from the ISF in recent days and weeks, will remain ineffective in producing the desired effect of seriously degrading the ISIS network.

To support operations in Iraq, there must be a second intelligence component— the collection and analysis effort of ISIS and their external support network must be made a priority for our National Intelligence Community. The ISIS network in

Iraq, Syria, and the regional support network external to the Iraq-Syria front must be a national collection and analysis priority. And one of the prime objectives of this collection is to identify and target ISIS finances and financial support. While ISIS is reported to be very well resourced from their recent asset seizures in Iraq, these resources must be replenished. We must identify all sources of income and employ all of the Counter Threat Finance tools that our Interagency brings to this fight in order to target and limit the free flow of funding to ISIS. This targeting must include any regional government and nongovernment entities.

Second, we should establish a training program for ISF to improve their basic combat skills to develop modest combined arms capability in order to effectively conduct offensive operations by conventional forces to dislodge ISIS from the occupied areas under ISIS control. The ISF are largely a "checkpoint army." Since 2011 their operations have been defensive in nature, static in disposition and disjointed in execution. They need training to develop the skills required to fight this ISIS army, as recent tactical failures against ISIS clearly indicate. We also need to enhance the capabilities of ISF Special Operations Forces. While these are the most competent and most effective of the ISF, they will need to greatly improve their capabilities in order to conduct the unrelenting, precise strike operations against critical ISIS targets.

Third, the ISF need assistance in establishing effective wartime sustainment structure and process. The existing sustainment system of the ISF is a peacetime system, designed to support fielding of military systems while dealing with a low-level insurgency. In 2010, we identified ISF sustainment as being a significant shortfall and that if it was not addressed, the readiness of ISF equipment would soon be in a "death spiral" where the backlog of deferred maintenance would overwhelm their abilities to field effective, modern forces. Reversing years of decline in equipment readiness will be a daunting, but not impossible process.

Fourth, The ISF require a decentralized command and control system that can rapidly process information and enable tactical decisions. The system that is in place in Iraq, one of Area Operations Commands emplaced by, and reporting directly to, Prime Minister Maliki, is a peacetime structure to ensure centralized control, with leaders chosen by the Prime Minister for loyalty over combat competence. The ISF require a command and control structure for sustained combat operations against a capable enemy.

Fifth, the ISF need the weaponry and equipment necessary for sustained combat operations. We have rushed some weapons and armaments to Iraq, however we need to do more. Most of our military aid to Iraq is moving at the glacial pace of our Foreign Military Sales (FMS) process. Iraq's Ambassador to the United States has lamented that the slow pace of our support when compared to the rapid support from Iran and Russia. We should quickly approve, ship, and enable material support to Iraq.

Sixth, we should support the ISF with airstrikes in order to degrade ISIS capabilities. But, let me be clear—isolated drone and air strikes in the absence of these other capabilities will be marginally effective. One cannot drone-strike or airstrike one's way out of this. These strikes will serve as an important part of a coordinated approach to this ISIS threat, but in isolation they will achieve fleeting effects. They must be integrated into the overall counteroffensive. Also, to produce effective airstrikes, especially against an enemy among the population, one needs to have air controllers on the ground to call in precise strikes and to control the effects. The Iraqis do not possess the capability to serve in this role. And no amount of isolated airstrikes will turn the current tactical situation in Iraq and produce decisive effects on their own.

Seventh, we should support the Kurds and enable them to defend against this existential threat of ISIS. The Peshmerga are an effective, determined and well-led force. However, they are lightly armed, inadequately equipped and insufficiently trained to counter the better-equipped ISIS force. They are stretched very thin over their 1,050-kilometer front with ISIS and, when ISIS turns on them, they will be outgunned and overmatched. The Kurds have proven to be loyal friends and allies to the United States and they have recently asked for material and nonmaterial support from us and we should expedite this support to them.

Understanding the complex relationship between Erbil and Baghdad, our "one Iraq" policy, and the arguments against aiding the Kurdish Region apart from the central government, the realities on the ground make this an exigent requirement. From a purely tactical and security perspective, why wouldn't we enable the Kurds to defend northern Iraq from ISIS, prevent the oil-rich north from falling into ISIS hands, and force ISIS to fight on two fronts in Iraq?

Security Depends on a Political Arrangement That Includes Sunnis and Kurds

However, for this security support to succeed, we need two things from Baghdad. First, we need a willing partner, one that is committed to accepting this assistance and to making the systemic and structural changes necessary to the Iraqi security structure in order to build the ISF into an effective force. Second, underpinning these military operations is the most critical requirement, a political accommodation of the Sunnis and the Kurds. In order to separate ISIS from their greatest advantage, an acquiescent Sunni population, there needs to be a political arrangement in Baghdad that the Sunnis can broadly accept. This political arrangement must also accommodate the Kurds and create the proper conditions for the Kurds to participate. However, as the recent political activities in Baghdad prove, a political agreement that satisfies all parties of Iraq could be the toughest impediment to reversing this existential threat to Iraq. But, in order for any hope of success, there must be some sort of political accommodation and an acceptable arrangement, which allows the Sunnis and Kurds to join in a unified military action.

CONCLUSION

ISIS is an existential threat to Iraq and a significant threat to the region. Iraq and its security forces have proven unable to defeat this threat in their present condition and with their present capabilities. The longer we wait to decide on our response to Iraq's requests for support, the stronger ISIS becomes. If the prevention of an ISIS-controlled Iraq is in the interest of the United States, then we should act to aid and enable Iraq and the Kurds to defeat this threat as quickly as possible.

Chairman Menendez, Ranking Member Corker, and distinguished members of the committee, again, thank you for the opportunity to appear before you today. I look forward to your questions.

Senator KAINE. Thank you, General Barbero.
Dr. Pollack.

STATEMENT OF KENNETH M. POLLACK, SENIOR FELLOW, SABAN CENTER FOR MIDDLE EAST POLICY, BROOKINGS INSTITUTE, WASHINGTON, DC

Dr. POLLACK. Mr. Chairman, Senator, it is always a great honor to appear before this committee.

I want to start by talking a little bit about some of the realities that we face in Iraq, because I think they are critical in understanding where we are and what the possibilities are moving forward. I want to just talk about two. First, we need to recognize that American influence in Iraq has attenuated very significantly, to the point where I would argue that at this point the United States interests exceed our influence.

Second, we need to come to grips with the fact that what we face in Iraq today is a civil war. Iraq is not on the brink, it is not sliding into it. It is a civil war, and the dynamics of intercommunal civil wars now apply, and those make intervention by third powers very difficult.

With that in mind, I think that the current approach of the administration, with a few tweaks, is probably the best one plausible. It is the only one, and that is the idea of forging a new political leadership and reforming Iraq's political system. It is the only option that we have that does offer the prospect of ending Iraq's civil war in a matter of months rather than years, and of preserving American interests in a whole variety of other ways.

But nevertheless, we need to recognize that it will be very difficult, and it goes well beyond merely replacing the current Iraqi political leadership. It is going to mean restructuring Iraq's politics in a way that will encompass the desires and aspirations and the fears of all of Iraq's communities, and that is not going to be easy.

If it fails, Iraq's civil war is going to roll on and, as I have already suggested, the dynamics of an intercommunal civil war were to take hold and those are very hard to break.

But we will have some options. Unfortunately, those options are all awful. I think the first one is to recognize, as any number of us and some of the Senators have made the point earlier, that Iraq and Syria are now a single civil war. And the problem that we will face in Iraq is that we will have a very complex situation. We will be looking to support both moderate Sunnis and moderate Shia against their extremists and hoping to forge a new peace between them. That is very hard.

Syria offers a little bit of clarity, in that we hate the regime, are not looking to support them in any way, and that at least opens up the prospect of developing a Syria-first policy, by which we would build a new Syrian opposition army that might be able to defeat both the regime and the extremists, stabilize the country, and serve as both a bridge and a model to Sunni moderates inside Iraq.

I see that option as entirely feasible, but it is not guaranteed to work and it is several steps beyond what the United States has been willing to consider so far. In fact, it will take years if it works at all and it will require a commitment of resources, probably including air power, that the United States has so far been unwilling to make.

If we are not willing to commit that level of resources to actually bring the civil war to a close, another option is partition, something that has been talked about very frequently. I will say that I think that if we do not bring this to a rapid close we will find that partition is the de facto outcome in Iraq. It will be divided up into a Sunnistan and a Shiastan and the Kurds will undoubtedly go their own way.

The question for us would be, can we find ways to turn de facto partition into de jure partition and somehow use it to bring about peace. Again, I think that is possible, but nevertheless it will be extremely difficult, far more difficult than I think many of its pundits and partisans around town are making it out to be. In fact, I would say that there is a dangerous mythology suggesting that partition of Iraq could be quick and easy and relatively bloodless.

In fact, Iraq's communities remain deeply intermingled. The different militias have made claims on territory currently held by the others. The fear that overwhelms Iraqis will remain and, what is more, dividing up Iraq's water, oil, and other resources will be enormously difficult. So the likelihood is that trying to bring about partition will take years and hundreds of thousands of lives lost.

The last alternative that we will have will be to follow a policy of containment, of trying to prevent the spillover from the Iraqi-Syrian civil war onto Iraq's other neighbors and from harming American interests in the region in that way. Again, this is certainly a possible alternative for the United States, but we need to remember that containment is exceptionally difficult. It has rarely succeeded in the past, and I think that the fall of Mosul is perhaps the most graphic illustration of just how hard it is to contain the spillover from one civil war from affecting another.

The last point I would make is simply that to do nothing would be the worst choice of all.

Thank you very much.

[The prepared statement of Dr. Pollack follows:]

PREPARED STATEMENT OF KENNETH M. POLLACK

Mr. Chairman and distinguished Senators, I am honored to be able to appear before you to discuss possible options to address the grave situation in Iraq.

I think it important to start any such conversation with an acknowledgement of the realities we face. First, it is painful, but necessary, to recognize that the United States has only very limited influence in Iraq today. The George W. Bush administration, by its many disastrous mistakes, squandered a great deal of the influence we once had there. The Obama administration, by its misguided neglect, surrendered most of what we had left. Indeed, Iraq now constitutes the hardest of situations for Americans to confront: it is a crisis in which our interests exceed our influence. Consequently, the options we consider moving forward must include methods to help increase U.S. influence to improve our ability to defend our interests.

Second, it is equally critical that we accept the reality that Iraq has fallen once more into civil war. It is not "on the brink of civil war." It is not "sliding into civil war." It is not "at risk of a new civil war." It is in a civil war. This is what civil war looks like. And civil wars have certain dynamics that need to be understood if they are to be ended, or even merely survived.

Iraq's current situation is the recurrence of the civil war of 2006–2008. In 2007–2008, the United States committed tremendous military and economic resources to pull Iraq out of that first instance of civil war. This time around, Washington has made clear that it will not devote anything like the same resources and there is no other country that can.

This second point is important because intercommunal civil wars like Iraq's are difficult for external powers to end without either a significant commitment of resources or a terrible slaughter by one or more of the combatants. Given the American public's understandable unwillingness to recommit the kind of resources we did in 2007–2008, we are unlikely to bring the Iraqi civil war to a speedy end with minimal bloodshed and still safeguard the range of American interests engaged there. For those reasons, the hard truth we face is that, in the circumstances we currently find ourselves in, our options range from bad to awful.

Nevertheless, doing nothing because all of the options are unpalatable would be the worst choice of all. Civil wars do not just go away if they are ignored. They burn on and on. They also have a bad habit of infecting neighboring states—just as the Syrian civil war has helped reignite the Iraqi civil war. If we try to turn our back on Iraq once again, it will affect its neighbors. It could easily affect the international oil market (and through it, the U.S. economy, which remains heavily dependent on the price of oil no matter how much we may frack). It will also generate terrorists who will seek to kill Americans. So our option may be awful, but we have no choice but to try to make them work.

PLAN A: REBUILDING A (SOMEWHAT) UNIFIED IRAQ

Although I believe that the Obama administration's Iraq policy has been disastrous, and a critical factor in the rekindling of Iraq's civil war,[1] I find myself largely in agreement with the approach they have adopted to deal with the revived civil war. Our first priority should be to try to engineer a new Iraqi Government that Kurds, Shia and moderate Sunnis can all embrace, so that they can then wage a unified military campaign (with American support) against ISIS and the other Sunni militant groups.[2]

That needs to remain Washington's priority until it fails because it is the best outcome for all concerned, including the United States. Doing so would be the most likely way to dampen or eliminate the current conflict, and create the fewest causes for future violence. It could also succeed relatively quickly—in a matter of months rather than years like all of the other options. However, it will be extremely difficult to pull off.

The keys to this strategy will be to convince the Kurds not to break from Iraq and convince moderate Sunnis to remain part of the Iraqi political process—and to turn on ISIS and the other Sunni militant groups. As I and other experts on Iraq have written, this will require both a new political leadership and a drastic overhaul of Iraq's political system. With regard to the former condition, at this point, it seems highly unlikely that Nuri al-Maliki can remain Prime Minister and retain either the Kurds or meaningful Sunni representation in his government. However, even if he were removed and new, more acceptable leaders chosen, there would still be a long way to go.[3]

Even moderate Sunni leaders are not going to go back to the status quo ante. They now insist on decentralizing power from the center to the periphery, a redistribution of power within the Federal Government, and a thorough depoliticization of the Iraqi security services so that they cannot be used as a source of repression by what will inevitably be a Shia-dominated central government. They are likely to demand to be allowed to form a federal region like the Kurdistan Regional Government, complete with a separate budget and their own military forces akin to the Kurdish Peshmerga.

For their part, the Kurds will want even more than that. At this point, given the extensive autonomy that the KRG already enjoys, coupled with the territorial and administrative gains it has won in the wake of the ISIS offensive, greater federalism probably won't be an adequate alternative to independence for the Kurds. If the Kurds can be prevented from seceding, it will probably require Baghdad to accept a confederal arrangement with Erbil.

The difference here is that in a typical federal system, resources and authorities are generated from the center and delegated to the periphery for all but a limited number of constrained functions. However, keeping the Kurds on board will likely necessitate a shift to one in which resources and authority begin in the periphery and then are shared with the center for specific purposes and under specific constraints.

The Kurds are likely to insist that the KRG maintain the current lines of control in disputed territories unchanged until a referendum can be conducted in accordance with article 140 of the Iraqi Constitution. Baghdad will have to recognize Erbil's right to develop and market the oil it produces as the new status quo. As for oil revenues, Erbil will demand that it be allowed to keep the Kirkuk oil fields it has now secured, and agree that Baghdad and Erbil each be allowed to pump as much oil as they like and pay all of their own expenses from those revenues.

Assuming that moderate Sunnis, Kurds and moderate Shia can all agree on these various changes, we could see the resurrection of a unified Iraqi polity. It is reasonable to assume that in those happy circumstances, many Sunni tribes will be ready to fight ISIS and the other Sunni militant groups—and to accept assistance from the United States to do so. (Although they have made clear that they will not accept assistance from the Iraqi Security Forces until they have been thoroughly depoliticized.) Moreover, these are really the only circumstances in which the United States should be willing to provide large-scale military assistance to the Iraqi Government to fight ISIS and the other militant groups. Only in those circumstances will such assistance be seen as nonpartisan, meant to help all Iraqis and not just the Shia (and their Iranian allies).

However, what is important to note about this scenario is that replacing Prime Minister Maliki, if that can be accomplished at all, is a necessary but not sufficient condition to end the conflict on the best terms imaginable for the United States (and Iraq). Even after Maliki is removed, the Iraqis will have to sort out far-reaching reforms and redistributions of power and wealth. As hard as all of that will be, there is the added danger that given the overwhelming distrust among all of the Iraqi parties, the Sunnis tribes will refuse to take any action against the Sunni militants until all of the political negotiations have been concluded. Having been burned so many times in the past, that will be a reasonable inclination on their part. However, if they do so, it could be months or years before they work things out and are ready to turn on ISIS and the other militants. By then it would be much harder to rid the country of the Sunni militants and those groups may well have done a great deal of damage already, including possibly mounting terrorist attacks abroad.

One area in which I think that the Obama administration could be doing a better job to foster this approach to the revived Iraqi civil war would be to lean in, rather than leaning back. What I mean by this is that moderate Iraqis from across the political and ethnosectarian spectrum have complained that while the administration is loudly demanding a wide range of changes in Iraq's political leadership and reforms of the Iraqi political process, they have so far been vague and equivocal in describing what the United States would do to help a new and reformed Iraqi Government. Given how many Iraqis already believe that President Obama wants nothing to do with Iraq and will never provide meaningful assistance, such reserve only undercuts what little influence the United States has left in Iraq.

Instead, the only way to increase American leverage with the Iraqis is to enumerate plainly the kinds of support that the United States would be willing to provide to a reformed, reunified Iraqi Government. This support should include drone strikes, the provision of weapons and reconnaissance assets, greater intelligence support and targeting assistance, improved and expanded training for Iraqi forces, and potentially even manned airstrikes. Better still, it could include a commitment to make the 2008 Strategic Framework Agreement into the kind of across-the-board bilateral assistance relationship always envisioned, but never actually implemented by the Obama administration. This would entail technical, administrative, and possibly even financial assistance for the full panoply of Iraqis needs—military, agriculture, education, energy, telecommunications, transportation, diplomatic, and virtually anything else the Iraqis might need. An American commitment to provide such assistance would be enormously popular among average Iraqis, and therefore would buy Washington considerable influence with their leaders. It would also galvanize Iraq's economy and help knit its fractured society back together—two more keys to preventing yet another outbreak of civil war.

PLAN B: SYRIA FIRST

If the United States, working in conjunction with our regional allies, the Iraqis themselves and (necessarily) the Iranians cannot forge a new Iraqi national consensus and power-sharing arrangement, the civil war will worsen.

Intercommunal civil wars like Iraq's share a number of unhelpful qualities. First, they tend to stalemate along the internal ethnosectarian dividing lines of the country. Those divides become the front lines, and they tend to be very, very bloody. Second, they tend to empower the worst elements in every society. It is the radicals who take advantage of the chaos and the fear, using it to kill off or drown out moderate rivals who are typically not ruthless enough to retain power. Of course, the radicals typically prosper from the conflict and have little interest in seeing it end except in complete victory.

Third, in part for that reason, intercommunal civil wars tend to burn on for years, sometimes even decades. The Algerian civil war ran from 1991 to 2002. The Lebanese civil war lasted from 1975–1991 and ended only because of Syrian intervention. The Congolese civil war has been roiling on since 1994. Somalia since 1991. Afghanistan has arguably careened from civil war to civil war since 1979, or more conventionally since 1989.

And fourth, they always produce spillover.[4] Spillover typically takes six different forms: terrorism, refugees, secessionism, radicalization of neighboring populations, economic downturns, and intervention by neighboring states. At its worst, spillover from an intercommunal civil war can help cause a civil war in another state (as spillover from Lebanon caused the 1976–1982 Syrian civil war, and the current Syrian civil war helped reignite the Iraqi civil war). Or it can metastasize into a regional war as neighboring states intervene to halt the other manifestations of spillover and/or to secure their interests against the predations of other states. That's how Israel and Syria came to blows over Lebanon in the 1980s and why seven different African states intervened in Congo, producing what is often referred to as "Africa's world war." For a variety of reasons, spillover from a protracted Iraqi civil war could be very bad, threatening U.S. allies like Turkey and Jordan and critical oil producers like Saudi Arabia, Kuwait, and Iran.

For all of these reasons, I believe that even if the current gambit fails, the United States will have a strong interest in seeing the civil war there ended. The problem, once again, is that doing so will be even harder with the limited resources that the U.S. is willing to employ. It will mean finding ways to appeal to both moderate Shia and moderate Sunnis in Iraq, help them to defeat their own radicals and then convince them to make peace with one another—and ideally forge a new power-sharing arrangement that would preserve a relatively unified Iraq. (Or a relatively unified Arab Iraq since it is highly unlikely the Kurds will refrain from independence under conditions of all-out civil war in Arab Iraq.)

Doing so in Iraq would probably mean starting in Syria. That may seem counterintuitive, but Syria offers an important clarity lacking in current Iraq. If Iraq is engulfed in full-scale civil war with no hope that political change in Baghdad could end the conflict, the United States will have a particularly problematic dilemma: we will have mixed feelings about both the Shia-dominated government and the Sunni-dominated opposition. We will hate ISIS and the Sunni radicals, but not the Sunni tribes and moderates allied with them. We will hate the Shia radicals and mistrust their Iranian allies, but not the Shia moderates who will inevitably have to join their coreligionists. Supplying both sides in any civil war is a nonstarter, but in Iraq those circumstances will make it (or should make it) impossible to decide which side to back. In that one respect, Syria is much easier. There the United States unequivocally backs the Sunni-dominated opposition against the Shia-dominated regime.

That situation would enable the United States to make a significantly greater effort to build a new, conventionally trained, armed, and organized Syrian opposition army. One that could defeat the forces of both the regime and the Sunni Islamist radicals.[5] Although such an effort would likely take anywhere from 2–5 years, it has a number of important advantages. First, it is entirely feasible—especially if coupled with Western air power. It would create the best conditions for a stable Syria, which would eliminate the spillover into Iraq, including the ability of ISIS and other radical groups to employ Syria as a base and recruiting ground to support operations in Iraq. Moreover, it would create a moderate, nonpartisan but largely Sunni force that could appeal to moderate Sunni tribesmen in Iraq. Indeed, a moderate, mostly Sunni, opposition army triumphing in Syria would be a tremendous draw for the Sunnis of Iraq—a model of what they might become if they rid themselves of ISIS, as well as an ally in that fight.

Finally, if the United States were to help create such a new model Syrian opposition army, one that could then serve as a conduit for American assistance to Iraqi Sunnis as well, Washington would then be ideally placed to reach out to moderate Shia groups in Iraq. The defeat of the Assad regime in Syria would doubtless terrify many Iraqi Shia that the Syrian opposition army planned to turn on them as well. As their trainers, advisors, paymasters, and weapons suppliers, the United States could then offer to rein in the new Syrian Army and even to provide similar assistance to moderate Iraqi Shia groups to enable them to defeat their own radicals. If they accepted, and they would have strong incentives to do so, they too would be beholden to the United States, creating the best circumstances possible for the U.S. to broker a deal between the moderate Sunnis and the moderate Shia (of both Iraq and Syria).

PLAN C: SEEKING A STABLE PARTITION

Building a new Syrian Army and helping it to defeat both the Assad regime and the Sunni militants would be time-consuming and require more resources than the U.S. has so far committed there, but it is hardly impossible. If we succeeded, then using that force to help Iraqi Sunnis turn on their own militants would also be a realistic aspiration. And if that too succeeded, then it is reasonable to believe that those circumstances could then be employed to convince Iraq's Shia to do the same. Finally making possible a negotiated settlement in Iraq.

Certainly there is no reason that any of this is impossible. But none of it will be easy. And each additional step adds degrees of time, cost, and difficulty. Even if we were willing to invest the time and resources to give this strategy the greatest likelihood of succeeding, it could take many years to seal the final deal. And there is no guarantee that every link in the chain would succeed enough to make the next link plausible.

With that in mind, I believe that the U.S. should also consider a more straightforward alternative, namely to try to end the fighting by convincing all sides to recognize the de facto division of the country that is likely to take place. As noted, the battle lines between Sunni and Shia militias are likely to run roughly along the blurry dividing lines between their communities. Tragically, those lines are likely to sharpen as a result of the widespread ethnic cleansing that will accompany the fighting and that has already begun again. The Kurds, will almost certainly opt for independence under these circumstances, and even if they refrain from a formal declaration, they will be independent in all but name.

In theory, a simpler alternative to trying to put Iraq back together again, would be to recognize its partition and convince the parties to accept that reality and stop fighting. Of course, what seems simple and obvious in theory often proves anything but that in practice.

Indeed, there is a dangerous mythology taking hold in Washington that partition might be easy because Iraq has since been sorted out into neat, easily divided cantonments. That is simply false. While there are far fewer mixed towns and neighborhoods, they still exist, and even the homogeneous towns and neighborhoods remain heavily intermingled across central Iraq, including in Baghdad. Moreover, both the Sunni and the Shia militias are claiming territory largely inhabited by the sects of the other. All of that indicates that it would probably take years of horrible bloodshed to convince both the Sunni and Shia leaderships to agree to partition, let alone on where to divide the country.

Thus, the challenge for the United States would be how to assist a process by which the various Iraqi factions recognized that continued fighting was fruitless and they should agree to a cease-fire and a functional division of the country to end the war altogether. That too will not be easy. Again, the key will be to empower moderates on both sides (Sunni and Shia) to enable them to defeat the radicals and then strike a workable deal with one another. (By definition, a moderate in an intercommunal civil war is someone willing to work with the other side.)

In theory, (there's that phrase again), the United States might provide military support to both Sunni and Shia moderates to help them triumph over their respective extremists in their respective cantonments. In practice, they are just as likely to try to use that assistance against each other as against the extremists. And if military assistance is not the right way to influence such groups waging an all-out civil war, it is even harder to imagine that any other form of assistance would have greater sway with them. Historically, only the threat of punishment has carried that kind of weight in such circumstances, but that would require a willingness on the part of the United States to become very heavily involved in the Iraqi civil war, quite possibly including with combat troops, which makes it a nonstarter.

Thus, the reality of a partition strategy is that, absent a willingness on the part of the U.S. to impose it by cracking heads, we will probably find ourselves on the sidelines, waiting and hoping that the Iraqi militia leaders will eventually recognize the futility of their combat and agree to accept Americans (or others) to step in as mediators and broker a disengagement and partition. That's not impossible. But typically, it is a long time coming, and in the meantime Iraqis will die while the region will suffer all of the effects of spillover. Partition may ultimately be the outcome in Iraq, but absent a plausible mechanism for the United States to convince the militias to agree to it in the near term, it will be difficult to adopt it is an actual strategy. As Colin Powell famously remarked, ''Hope is not a strategy,'' and hoping that Iraqi militia leaders recognize the error of their ways is not a good way to safeguard American interests in the region.

PLAN D: CONTAINMENT

Inevitably, America's last option would be containment.[6] We could simply opt to leave Iraq to its fate and try as best we might to block or mitigate the spillover onto its neighbors. In fact, unless and until we could find a way to convince the militias to stop fighting, the ''partition'' approach described above would have to rely on containment. To some extent, so too would a strategy of remaking Iraqi politics by building a new Syrian opposition army that could stabilize Syria and then help stabilize Iraq since that would be a long time in the making if it succeeded at all. In short, the United States is probably going to rely on at least some aspects of a containment strategy toward Iraq under any circumstances unless we are able to help forge a new Iraqi political leadership and power-sharing agreement that stops the civil war in its tracks.

The problem with containment is that it does not work very well. Historically, few nations have been able to stave off the worst aspects of spillover from an intercommunal civil war for very long. Most countries find themselves suffering worse and worse, and often getting drawn into the civil wars the longer they drag on. It is harder to find good cases of neighboring countries that successfully minimized the impact of spillover on themselves.

In many cases states have simply tried to weather the storm and paid a heavy price for doing so. Others have been driven to do what they could to end the conflict instead. Syria spent at least 8 years trying to end the Lebanese civil war before the 1989 Ta'if accords and the 1990–91 Persian Gulf War gave it the opportunity to finally do so. Israel's 1982 invasion was also a bid to end the Lebanese civil war after its previous efforts to contain it had failed, and when this too failed Jerusalem tried to go back to managing spillover. By 2000, it was clear that this was again ineffective and so Israel simply pulled out of Lebanon altogether in a vain effort to prevent further spillover. Withdrawing from Lebanon was smart for Israel for many reasons, but it has not put an end to its Lebanon problem. In the Balkans, the United States and its NATO Allies realized that it was impossible to manage the Bosnian or Kosovar civil wars and so in both cases they employed coercion—including the deployment of massive ground forces—to bring them to an end. Pakistan opted to try to end the Afghan civil war by building and encouraging the Taliban, an effort that, 20 years later, has left Pakistan riven by internal conflict of its own.

Nevertheless, we may well have nothing left but to try to contain the spillover from an Iraqi civil war. From America's perspective that will require pursuing a number of critical courses of action.

Provide Whatever Assistance We Can to Iraqi Civilians and Refugees. In this scenario Iraq's civil war will rage on, fueled by its militias and, unfortunately, its neighbors. The biggest losers will be the people of Iraq themselves. Hundreds of thousands are likely to die. Millions will be forced to flee their homes and suffer other tragedies. Those people represent both a moral responsibility and a strategic threat since they constitute ideal recruitment pools for militias and terrorists. Especially if the United States opts not to do anything to try to bring the civil war to a rapid end, but also if we are merely forced to wait for other aspects of our strategy to gain traction, we should and must provide what support we can to the people of Iraq, both those who remain and those who flee. Undoubtedly various international NGOs and U.N. agencies will do what they can, but without the resources of nation-states, they will not be able to do much.

Provide Support to Iraq's Neighbors. The historical evidence from other intercommunal civil war suggests that the United States should provide assistance to Iraq's neighbors to reduce the likelihood that their own deprivation will create sympathy for, or incite emulation of, the actions of their compatriots in Iraq. The more content the people of neighboring states, the less likely they will be to want to get involved in someone else's civil war. Aid also provides some leverage with the government in question, making them more likely to hesitate before going against U.S. wishes. Generous aid packages can be explicitly provided with the proviso that they will be stopped (and sanctions possibly applied instead) if the receiving country intervenes in the Iraqi conflict.

That would mean continuing and even expanding the roughly $660 million in aid the United States is providing Jordan this year. It will probably mean increased assistance to Turkey to help it deal with both refugees and terrorism emanating from the intertwined Iraqi-Syrian civil wars.

The more difficult questions will be how to help Kuwait and Saudi Arabia. Neither Kuwait nor Saudi Arabia need American financial assistance, although both might need greater security cooperation to deal with terrorists and militiamen spilling over their borders in search of either targets or sanctuary.

However, the bigger problem that both Kuwait and Saudi are likely to face will be the radicalization of their populations, a problem both were beginning to face in 2006 before the U.S. "Surge" shut down the first manifestation of civil war in Iraq. Saudi and Kuwaiti Shia minorities will doubtless sympathize with—and be galvanized by—the Shia of Iraq and Syria. Their Sunni majorities will side with the Sunni oppositions in both and will demand that their governments do ever more to support the Sunni fighters. It will almost certainly lead to widespread gulf covert support to the Sunni militias in Iraq and Syria, potentially including ISIS and the other militant groups. Historically, such covert support can backfire against the country providing the support, as Pakistani support for the Taliban, Jordanian support for the PLO, and Turkish support for the Syrian opposition has. It can also lead to conventional interventions into the civil war when the covert support proves inadequate to the task. That's how Syria and Israel got sucked into Lebanon.

Dissuade Intervention. Consequently, the United States, hopefully along with its European and Asian allies, will have to make a major effort to convince Iraq's neighbors not to intervene in an Iraqi civil war. Given the extent of their involvement already, this will be difficult to do. Our efforts should include the economic aid described above, as well as specific benefits tailored to the needs of individual countries. For Jordan and Saudi Arabia it might be yet another quixotic tilt at an Israeli-Palestinian peace, thereby addressing another of their major concerns. For Turkey, it might be financial aid or NATO security assistance. Again, Saudi Arabia and Kuwait would be the biggest challenges and the best Washington might do would be merely to try to convince them that it would be counterproductive and unnecessary to intervene—unnecessary because the U.S. and its allies will make a major effort to keep Iran from intervening, which will be their greatest worry.

Preventing Iran from intervening, especially given how much it is already involved in Iraqi affairs, is going to be the biggest headache of all. Given Iran's immense interests in Iraq, deepening Iranian intervention is likely to go hand in hand with a worsening civil war. And that is a foregone conclusion in a scenario of containment. For Tehran, the United States may have to lay down "redlines" regarding what is absolutely impermissible—like sending uniformed Iranian military units into Iraq or annexing Iraqi territory, both of which could prompt the Sunni Arab states to do the same. Of course, the U.S. and its allies would also have to lay out what they would do to Iran if it were to cross any of those redlines and that will inevitably be complicated by the status of nuclear negotiations with Tehran, regardless of the status of those negotiations.

Direct Strikes at the Terrorist Infrastructure in Iraq. If the United States opts merely to contain an Iraqi civil war, we will have to accept some level of terrorist activity there. However, we would have to try to limit the ability of terrorists (Sunni and possibly Shia as well) to use Iraq as a haven for attacks outside the country. That will mean reliance on the kind of approach that Vice President Biden purportedly favored in Afghanistan rather than the "surge" of troops that President Obama opted for instead. It would mean employing air assets (manned and unmanned), special operations forces, and all manner of intelligence and reconnaissance systems to identify and strike key terrorists and their infrastructure (training camps, bomb factories, arms caches, etc.) before they could pose a danger to Americans. Thus, the

U.S. would continue to make intelligence collection in Iraq a high priority, and whenever such a facility was identified, Shia or Sunni, American forces would move in quickly to destroy it.

Of course, such an effort would need bases to operate. Jordan and Kuwait are obvious candidates. However, in this scenario, Iraqi Kurdistan would probably be the best of all. Indeed, the United States could tie its willingness to recognize an independent Kurdistan (and provide them with the kind of military support they will need to hold off Iran as well as ISIS and the Sunni Arab militant groups) to Erbil's willingness to host American counterterrorism (CT) forces. It seems highly likely that the Kurds would jump at that opportunity, making it far more palatable to run a discrete CT campaign from independent Iraqi Kurdistan than anywhere else.

LEARNING THE LESSON OF IRAQ

Mr. Chairman, as I reflect on the list of options I have described above, I find myself deeply depressed. This is a miserable set of choices. But they reflect the reality of our circumstances in Iraq.

Whatever options we choose to pursue there, I find myself hoping that at the very least, we will recognize that the best option of all was to have never allowed ourselves and the Iraqis to get to this point. They have been sucked into a civil war that feeds upon itself, and we are left with almost nothing we can do, either to save them or prevent that maelstrom from wrecking vital American interests. The mistakes of both the Bush '43 and Obama administrations led us to this point because neither was willing to acknowledge that we cannot break a country in a vital part of the world and then walk away from it. And neither was willing to practice the sage aphorism that an ounce of prevention is worth a pound of cure. Today we have but an ounce of cure for a malady raging out of control, one that could easily kill the patient and who knows what else. Perhaps the best that might come of it would be if we learn not to do so again.

Notes

[1] This should not be taken to imply that I believe Iraq's current problems are entirely the fault of the Obama administration. Quite the contrary. I believe that the George W. Bush administration is at least equally to blame, and arguably more so.

[2] Full disclosure: I proposed that the United States adopt this policy the day after Mosul fell and before the administration embraced it. See Kenneth M. Pollack, "How to Pull Iraq Back from the Abyss," The Wall Street Journal, June 10, 2014.

[3] For a fuller description of the political reforms that would be required to make this scenario work, see Zalmay Khalilzad and Kenneth M. Pollack, "How to Save Iraq," The New Republic Online, July 22, 2014.

[4] On spillover from intercommunal civil wars, its causes, manifestations and efforts to stem it, see Daniel L. Byman and Kenneth M. Pollack, "Things Fall Apart: Containing the Spillover from an Iraqi Civil War" (Washington, DC: The Brookings Institution, 2006).

[5] For a fuller description of this strategy, see Kenneth M. Pollack, "An Army to Defeat Assad: How to Turn Syria's Opposition into a Real Fighting Force," forthcoming, Foreign Affairs, Vol. 93, No. 5 (September/October 2014). Also see, Daniel L. Byman, Michael Doran, Kenneth M. Pollack and Salman Shaikh, "Saving Syria: Assessing Options for Regime Change," Middle East Memo No. 21, The Saban Center for Middle East Policy at the Brookings Institution, March 15, 2012.

[6] For more on the methodologies of containment, see Byman and Pollack, "Things Fall Apart," op. cit.

The CHAIRMAN [presiding]. Well, thank you all for your testimony. I am sorry I had to step out, but we had the benefit of having your testimony in advance.

Let me ask you, Ambassador Jeffrey, if Maliki is the problem and Maliki somehow rises to be Prime Minister again, what is the course of events for us?

Ambassador JEFFREY. First of all, it is not going to be easy for him to hang on as Prime Minister, because he will need the votes, as Mr. McGurk said, of at least part of the Sunni community and part of the Kurdish community to get above the 165 that is needed. What I fear is that there will be a long delay, and that is what we had in 2010, where he will be the Acting Prime Minister for many months and people will get more discouraged.

So I think the first thing is for us to press for this process to go forward, because I think that most Iraqis, including many of the Shia parties, do believe that they need a new leader. If he does stay in power, then our options are far more along the lines that Dr. Pollack has suggested at the end, of containing the problem and dealing with Iraq and Syria from Jordan, from Kurdistan, with Turkey to the extent that is possible, to try to both contain the danger and go after some of these ISIL elements that we think are threatening us or threatening the stability of the region.

It will be very hard to work with a government in Baghdad that does not have the buy-in of the Sunnis and the Kurds, and it will not be possible to assist in any retakeover of those Sunni areas by an army that does not represent the people of the region.

The CHAIRMAN. And if the flip side of that happens, that in fact he does not continue as Prime Minister, what are the immediate things that the next government will have to do in order to create the type of national unity that can fight ISIS and not have the country disintegrate?

Ambassador JEFFREY. I have my own list. We all have lists, and frankly the Iraqis have their lists as well, Mr. Chairman. But a few things are crucial. First of all, to keep the Kurds in there has to be a deal. Brett McGurk—on oil. Brett McGurk talked about some of the options. He has negotiated a lot of them—they are ready, they are on the shelf—that would give them a bigger slice of over-all resources while bringing them back into the system. That is very important.

There needs to be real revenue-sharing. They already have tried this. Up until recently, the Kurds were getting 17 percent. Some of the either oil-producing provinces—Basra, Kirkuk—or those with a lot of pilgrims—Najaf—were getting slices of the Iraqi central government budget to execute their own programs, and they were very, very successful, particularly in Najaf and Kirkuk. So there is a model also on the shelf to have more economic federalism.

So it is not just lists of things. If you want inclusiveness you get rid of the guy who represents a lack of inclusiveness. That will do more than any action plan. If you want to have economic fed-eralism, then you introduce financial and energy policies that will see to that. And if you want to have a security force that is capable of doing what General Barbero said, let us have a new Defense Minister who actually does have command and control over his forces, which is not the case now.

The CHAIRMAN. Dr. Pollack, do you have anything to add?

Dr. POLLACK. I would just add one point to, I think, the excellent points that Ambassador Jeffrey just raised, which is that I think the United States needs to do a lot more to put on offer to the Iraqis, to make clear what we would do to help them if they actu-ally took the steps that we are looking for. Right now my sense from Iraqis is we are demanding a great deal from them, but we are not actually letting them know what we would do for them if they took what are actually very difficult steps for them.

That gets to Ambassador Jeffrey's point about how we need to be pressuring them, how we need to be pushing this process forward. Getting rid of Prime Minister Maliki is going to be very difficult and I think the Iraqis need to understand in much more concrete terms, rather than the more vague promises that they seem to be hearing, at least that they are hearing, from the administration about what they would get if they did it.

The CHAIRMAN. General Barbero, I am really hesitant to continue to authorize sales or to approve sales—it is up to the administration to authorize them, but to approve sales—when I have seen what has happened so far with some very critical armament that has fallen to the hands of ISIS as a result of it being abandoned on the battlefield. So how, in light of your comments that we need to respond to Iraqis' requests for help, which I assume in part is possibly air strikes, but also they are looking for equipment, how do we create the safeguards so that if we are going to help we do not end up having our weaponry fall in the hands of ISIS and used against the very forces that we want to defeat them?

General BARBERO. Mr. Chairman, as you look at every conflict there has been—it is not an antiseptic environment where—you will have loss of equipment. It just will happen.

The CHAIRMAN. But not to the tune that——

General BARBERO. Not to the tune that we had, not with the rout in Mosul, I agree, and I share your concern and dismay over that. I think from this assessment we look at which are the good units of the Iraqi Security Forces and we invest heavily in them with advice, training, whatever they need, and then take a hard look at what they have asked for and what we are willing to share with them and make some decisions.

But a senior Iraqi military leader last week said to me: Where is America? The Russians are performing and supporting us. The Iranians are here. We want the Americans. You are our friends.

They are frustrated. We can ship all the Hellfires we want. They have three fixed-wing aircraft to fire Hellfires. It sounds great, briefs well. You cannot, as I said, air strike your way out of this.

So I would pick the right units from this assessment and I would invest in them with the weapons and equipment that we feel that would help.

The CHAIRMAN. Well, I would say to the Iraqis, billions of dollars, hundreds of lives, that is where America has been. And I would also remind them that they were unwilling to pursue a status of forces agreement which might have created the wherewithal to continue to solidify the Iraqi Security Forces. So I think they have to think about the decisions that they have made, not to relive them, but to instruct them moving forward.

Senator Corker.

Senator CORKER. Thank you, Mr. Chairman.

Again, thank you for being here. I think a lot of times our second panels are actually better than the first, but by that time people have other business. You are more independent voices, and again we thank you so much for your help.

Dr. Pollack, you responded, facially anyway, when Senator Menendez just mentioned that they were unwilling to pursue a status of forces agreement. I was just wondering what you were hoping to say, but did it instead with an expression?

Dr. POLLACK. I think that what was going through my head, Senator, was that that was a moment when I think both the United States and Iraq both failed each other and themselves. It was a moment when I think that Prime Minister Maliki was at best ambivalent about whether or not he wanted an American presence, which history has proven would have been beneficial to him. And I think that it was a time when the United States was ambivalent at best about whether or not it wanted to stay, and I think that history has once again proven that it would have been better had we done so.

Senator CORKER. I know our focus needs to be on the future, but I know Ambassador Jeffrey had sort of a give and take publicly in writing with folks regarding this. Is that your impression of what happened during that time, just very briefly? I want to move on to some other things.

Ambassador JEFFREY. Very briefly, the administration, following the recommendation of its military leaders and my recommendation, in 2010 offered to keep troops on. In essence, the Maliki government and most of the political parties except the Sadrists agreed to have troops. We got hung up on the question of a status of forces agreement. Maliki was reluctant to do this. Iyad Allawi, who controlled the Sunnis in Parliament, said that he would not move any further than Maliki would move. That undercut how we had done the deal back in 2008 when we had gotten the earlier agreement, and, frankly, time ran out.

In terms of how enthusiastic the administration was about it, I had my instructions, which were to try to get an agreement.

Senator CORKER. I notice—thank you both for that clarification— that there has been sort of a discussion of the order of steps that need to take place, and there has been a heavy emphasis on getting the right political situation. I think all of you agree with that. Some of you would like to see us go ahead and take some steps now.

Let me ask you, General, what do you think—what are some of the elements of debate that are taking place now relative to, if you were guessing—and my guess is you actually talk with some of these people from time to time—prior to us knowing if they are going to have an inclusive government, someone other than Maliki, what do you think are some of the elements of the debate that are taking place inside the administration relative to taking some small steps, not something sustained, but some of those small steps that I think you have mentioned might build morale at a minimum and maybe stave off some of the steps that ISIL is taking?

General BARBERO. I think there has been a reliance on this, as Ms. Slotkin said, a very deliberate process, in a very exigent situation. This process has in my view become a way to not take action, and we are in a situation where ISIS, as I said, is an existential threat to Baghdad, the Kurds, and in the region, and they are gaining strength.

I think there has been discussion of air strikes, and you can take air strikes on targets without having precision if you see these entities out in the desert. That will only be for fleeting effects. It must be part of a sustained effort. So just doing air strikes or drone strikes can have some effect, but it will not be lasting or decisive.

I think there is great reluctance to reintroduce American Forces. I get that. I understand. But if this is an existential threat, if, as we have heard, it is in the national interest of the United States, this situation, and if the Iraqi Security Forces are the way to deal with this, and these Iraqi Security Forces are not prepared or capable of dealing with it, then it is a dichotomous situation. You cannot close that circle without some external assistance to these forces.

So I hope it is not a question of if we should support the Iraqi Security Forces and introduce the steps that I said; it is a question of when and, now that we have had this assessment, how quickly.

Senator CORKER. So the fear would be paralysis through purposeful long-term analysis. That would be the fear, just analyzing this forever and not taking action.

I also agree with you there is some reticence to get back involved too militarily. But things are dissipating quickly.

Let me ask you this. Maliki obviously, he may not have been a good Prime Minister, but he understands the debate that is taking place in our country and knows that him being gone, while we might not have laid out as clearly—and I think it is a great comment from you for us to share with them specifically what we would do if they had this inclusive government. I think that is a great point.

But can you tell if there is any leveraging taking place by Maliki right now, knowing that we are not going to get involved in any kind of big way if he is still there? Is there any activity that is occurring there relative to him trying to leverage us in other ways?

Ambassador JEFFREY. Dr. Pollack might have information as well. I think that, first of all, he points out correctly that he did very well in the last elections several months ago, winning personally 700,000 votes, which was even more than he did in 2010. His party came in first. Under the constitution, he should be given by the new President selected today within 15 days an opportunity to form a government. And under the constitutional process, if he cannot form it—and I think it will be hard for him to form it—after 30 days the mandate has to pass to another party.

Now, that is a lot of time to consume doing this. I think that as a minimum he is going to want to play this out. He also may feel that in the end the Americans, having sent, what was it, 775 additional forces to Iraq, are ready to help them out regardless of what happens. Again, I think I and many others have said under certain circumstances right now striking ISIL where they pose a danger is important, but we cannot provide the whole gamut, the whole breadth of support that they need absolutely unless we have an inclusive government that can bring in the Sunnis and bring in the Kurds, and it will not happen with him, sir.

Senator CORKER. Just one last question. I know my time is up and I know all of us probably have to be places. But I know there is discussion—and you have said this—about this being a regional approach and Syria and Iraq obviously having no border between them any more. What are some of the dynamics on the Syrian side that as we look at this regionally—I know you are just focused on Iraq now—that complicate, with Assad being in power there, complicate our ability to look at it regionally?

Dr. POLLACK. I am glad to start, Senator. I think one of the most obvious problems is the one that I have already mentioned, which is that when you look only at Syria we look at it and we say, we do not like the Assad regime, we want it gone, therefore the question is simply how best to help the opposition. When we look at Iraq we have a situation where you have a Shia group in charge of the government, they are likely to remain in charge of the government, and we are going to want to maintain good ties with them. Simultaneously, we have got a Sunni opposition that includes some people we really dislike—ISIS and the militants—and others who we very much like. So there is a complexity that is involved, and therefore any support to one of these groups becomes complicated by the opposite effect that it has with the other.

So if we are providing enormous support to Sunni oppositionists in Syria, inevitably some of that support is going to flow to opposition—to Sunni groups in Iraq, some of whom we may not like. The more that we are helping the Maliki government in Baghdad, the more it is going to be seen by folks in the region as supporting the wider Shia cause, which also encompasses the Assad government.

Obviously, that is only the tip of the iceberg. There is a lot more to talk about. But we do need to recognize the complexity that has now been introduced into this situation by having simultaneously civil wars in Iraq and Syria that are by and large merged, which the region sees in a very simple way as a Sunni-Shia fight, but which we see in a much more complex way.

Senator CORKER. Would anybody like to add to that?

General BARBERO. If I could, Senator. As far as a regional approach, we know that ISIS is—they are awash in money. But the way to choke these organizations is to go after their financing. Now, for the near term they have got plenty of that. However, we know there are regional actors supporting them, supporting ISIS, and we should employ, as I said in my statement, our intelligence community to identify those actors and then use every tool we have in the interagency—Department of Commerce, Department of Treasury—to go after those actors and these sources of funding.

We know, have a good idea, where it is coming from. Let us identify them and target them as part of a regional approach to this growing problem.

Senator CORKER. Thank you, Mr. Chairman.

Thank you all for being here.

The CHAIRMAN. One last set of questions. General, you served in Iraq. You led our mission to train and equip Iraqi Forces. When U.S. Forces left Iraq it seemed that Iraqi Forces were on their way to becoming a capable force. So that begs the question: What happened? Why did the ISF's capability and capacity erode so quickly?

General BARBERO. Senator, tough question, and it is tough to see what has happened, and it is tough to see what has been happening over the last few years. I have been back to Iraq many times over the last year since I left active duty.

But the ISF was built to handle a low-level insurgency and our goal was to get them to a state where they were good enough. Frankly, when I was there in 2009 and 2010 and into 2011, the assumption we had as we did our development plan, there would be a residual force of advisers and trainers to continue this development. I did an assessment in the summer of 2010 for then-General Odierno, which we briefed to everyone in Iraq and every Iraqi leader, saying: Here is where your forces are going to be in December

2011. We wanted to convince them and show them the capabilities and the shortfalls of their forces.

The shortfalls we identified, some were very obvious. They could not control their own air space nor defend it. But we said: You have a sustainment problem, your military readiness of your equipment is in a death spiral. Unless you do something very seriously, you will not be able to field an army. Your command and control structure is not workable. This peacetime for command and control of the population directly to the Prime Minister, it has to change. You do not have an NCO corps.

What I think most fundamentally is, we told the Iraqis: You must invest in training. Good armies train continuously. And we did not see that before we left and I have not seen any evidence of that since then.

So the short answer is the development that needed to take place with the Iraqi Security Forces from December 2011 to July 2014 has not taken place. We can go back and forth about advisers and trainers, but they just have not developed as they should.

The CHAIRMAN. So if that is the case, then what will advisers now be able to do at this stage that will make a difference on the ground with Iraqi Forces?

General BARBERO. Well, when we were on the ground with them and advising and training, it did make a difference. I think first we can stop the bleeding. They are under severe duress with the VBIED campaign that has started in Baghdad. Indirect fire is coming. ISIS is not going to let up. So if this is in our interest, then we need to get something in there to help them, A, stop the bleeding, and then start building these forces.

But this will not take weeks or months. This is going to take a while to get them to a state—as I said in my comments, unless we have an Iraqi Government that is willing to accept these changes and willing to emplace these changes into their structure and the way they do business, then I would question whether we should do it.

The CHAIRMAN. Two last questions. Can air strikes alone—I think you alluded to this in your answer to one of Senator Corker's questions. But can air strikes alone make a difference in pushing back ISIS, or would doing them now just be in essence giving the Iraqis a boost?

General BARBERO. Air strikes can make a difference, tactical difference. They can help enable Iraqi Forces. They can help relieve pressure. They can help degrade ISIS capabilities. But my point is we cannot think that just through air strikes and drone strikes we can solve this problem or, I would argue, even hold it in abeyance. They would make a difference. It would not be a decisive difference.

The CHAIRMAN. So the flip, the other side of this, then is training and assisting Iraqi Forces, can they possibly recover the country, even with the training and assisting?

General BARBERO. I think they could.

The CHAIRMAN. You think they could?

General BARBERO. I think they could.

The CHAIRMAN. We are talking about what period of time?

General BARBERO. Months. It is not going to happen overnight.

Ambassador JEFFREY. Senator, if I could support General Barbero. I have seen it myself. I was in Vietnam as an Army officer in 1972. The South Vietnamese Army, when the North Vietnamese regular army invaded for the first time, they started melting worse than Mosul. Millions, billions of dollars of U.S. equipment was lost within days. Then when we started air strikes it changed the psychology of those forces almost overnight, and within 3 months they had recovered almost the entire country.

We saw in Libya, we saw in Kosovo, and we saw in Bosnia where air strikes can provide lightly equipped, sometimes not too well trained forces the difference in taking on better equipped forces. As Brett McGurk I think three times described earlier today, dealing with the Shamar Tribe up near Mosul, dealing with the people, and I know Governor Delami is still holding out in Ramadi, a Sunni governor, against ISIL, they are outgunned. He described how they had volunteers to go into northern Fallujah, but they lost in a battle to ISIL because the ISIL people were better equipped and better trained.

So a combination of air strikes and advisers, not boots on the ground, can make a huge difference, sir.

The CHAIRMAN. One last question for you, General. Are you surprised by the alarming reports of Iraqi Security Forces' abuses, infiltration by Shia militias, and lack of accountability? And how do we engage with the Iraqi Forces to deal with those challenges?

General BARBERO. Senator, I was in Erbil and Baghdad in late May, so the developments in Mosul and what has happened after that I think was a shock in Mosul and Baghdad and Washington. I was shocked by it.

But as I drive around Baghdad or Basra or other places over the last year, it is a checkpoint army. I have said that. You cannot take on an ISIS if you have been in static positions on the defense and not trained for offensive operations.

What is troubling is as you ride up to these army checkpoints there are Shia religious banners almost at every one across Baghdad, certainly in Basra. So there must be a fundamental change in the nature of these forces, not only the government, but the forces, to allow participation by Sunni and Kurds in this unified effort that it would require.

The CHAIRMAN. Well, I appreciate your insights. I am not a military guy, but I will say that when an American soldier volunteers, he fights for a cause, for a principle, for a set of values, and he fights for his nation, he or she fights for their nation. If the job is just a job, then it does not turn out the same way. And it is difficult to get an Iraqi Army if you do not feel you are fighting for the totality of a country—Shia, Sunni, and Kurd. And that is a real problem.

Anyhow, I appreciate all of your insights as we grapple with the choices we have to make.

This record will remain open until the close of business tomorrow. With the thanks of the committee, this hearing is adjourned.

[Whereupon, at 12:42 p.m., the hearing was adjourned.]

―――――――

ADDITIONAL MATERIAL SUBMITTED FOR THE RECORD

RESPONSE OF BRETT MCGURK TO QUESTION SUBMITTED BY SENATOR TIM KAINE

Question. The Islamic State (formerly ISIS) is among the most well-financed terrorist organizations in the world, with financial flows running into tens of millions of dollars. Please describe the status of Islamic State finances, including internal sources (oil revenue, taxes, smuggling) as well as any external flows and what the U.S is doing to counter IS financing.

Answer. The Islamic State of Iraq and the Levant (ISIL) derives the majority of its financing from criminal activities including smuggling, robberies, extortion, and kidnapping for ransom, as well as raiding villages and towns. ISIL controls some smaller oil and gas fields, pipelines, and related infrastructure in Iraq, but not Iraq's major oil fields, which are in territory under the control of the Government of Iraq in the south and the Kurdish Regional Government forces in the north. ISIL receives some money from outside donors, but that pales in comparison to its self-funding through criminal and terrorist activities.

The issue of preventing private financing of violent extremists remains an important priority in our discussions with all states in the region. We are working closely with our partners in the region to halt the sale of ISIL-sourced oil, and prevent external financial support for terrorists from crossing their borders.

The United States and other key players in the international financial system pay extremely close attention to the risks associated with terrorist financing. We approach these issues with partners in the global financial system, such as the intergovernmental Financial Action Task Force, with financial regulators, and with financial institutions and their compliance officers.

———

RESPONSES OF BRETT MCGURK TO QUESTIONS
SUBMITTED BY SENATOR JEFF FLAKE

Question. The administration has blamed Baghdad for not heeding U.S. warnings about ISIL's impending advance into Mosul.

♦(a) Was it a surprise when ISIL took control over Fallujah earlier this year?

Answer. We have maintained a close watch on Iraq's security situation since the stand-up of the U.S. Embassy in Baghdad in 2004. The threat of the Islamic State of Iraq and the Levant (ISIL) and its effect on Iraq's overall security situation was neither a surprise nor a sudden event. We have watched and warned of ISIL's growing strength and its threat to Iraq and U.S. interests in the region—and now to Europe and the U.S. homeland—since the group's resurgence in 2012, largely due to the escalating conflict in Syria.

♦(b) Did the administration warn Baghdad or share intelligence with officials there preceding the ISIL takeover of Fallujah?

Answer. The Government of Iraq has long been aware of the threat that ISIL poses, and during Prime Minister Maliki's meetings in Washington last fall the need to develop a holistic strategy to counter its rise was a topic of discussion at several of PM Maliki's meetings with USG officials. As the ISIL threat increased, we took several steps to increase counterterrorism assistance with Iraq and to build a foundation for future, expanded cooperation. We enhanced information-sharing relationships, expanded training in Iraq and Jordan, provided military advice, and sought opportunities to increase border security. After the withdrawal of U.S. Forces in 2011, we maintained a close partnership with Iraq's military intelligence, Directorate General for Intelligence and Security, and other intelligence agencies across the government and Ministry of Defense. Information and intelligence-sharing has been and remains crucial to the fight against ISIL.

♦(c) How long has ISIL been of concern to the administration?

Answer. From the moment this administration took office, ISIL—formerly Al Qaeda in Iraq (AQI)—has been a concern. This organization has posed a threat since the Bush administration when it was known as Al Qaeda in Iraq under the direction of Zarqawi. Since the start of the Syrian conflict, we watched with growing concern as ISIL took advantage of the escalating war to establish a safe-haven in Syria's eastern desert. With ample resources, recruits, weapons, and training, ISIL slowly began to execute its strategy to create an Islamic caliphate across the Syrian border into Iraq. Violence in Iraq began to increase toward the end of 2012, but did not gain momentum until early 2013, with a marked rise in ISIL suicide bombings. Taking advantage of the instability it was causing, ISIL then seized parts of Anbar province, including the cities of Ramadi and Fallujah, in early January 2014. The Government of Iraq then initiated a concerted counterterrorism campaign against ISIL, which has continued to this day. Although ISIL has long operated in Mosul and northern Iraq, its sudden, large-scale offensive there in June escalated the fight, dramatically demonstrating the existential threat to Iraq posed by ISIL.

Question. The United States has sat back and watched while ISIL took control of Fallujah, Mosul, Tikrit, and moved into Diyala province. The U.S. has sent 300 advisors to Iraq and air strikes remain an option still under review. According to CRS, ''U.S. officials express increasing confidence that the IS-led offensive will not be able to capture [Baghdad] outright, although the ISF might yet lose parts of the city.''

♦(a) What are the administration's goals in Iraq? What does it hope to achieve with the sending of advisors to aid the ISF?
♦(b) Are we content with letting ISIL maintain control over the territory it's already claimed?

Answer. Our goals in Iraq remain promoting the emergence of a safe, peaceful, and politically inclusive state, which supports our approach for regional security. Iraq needs to move forward quickly to assemble a new government that will respect the rights, aspirations, and legitimate concerns of all Iraqis. We are in constant communication with Iraq's leaders, urging them to come together and take a united stand against violent extremism.

We also are exploring more ways to assist the Iraqi Security Forces in the battle against ISIL. Over the last 6 months, we surged U.S. diplomatic, intelligence, and military resources to develop strategic options supported by real-time and accurate information. More recently, a team of U.S. military advisors conducted an assessment of the Iraqi Security Forces, which we will use to determine of how we can best assist the Iraqis in the ongoing fight.

As Secretary Kerry remarked in June, supporting Iraq in its struggle against violent extremism supports our strategic interests and responsibilities, including providing security for the American people, fighting terrorism, and standing by our allies. We will do what is necessary and what is in our national interest to confront ISIL and the threat that it poses to the security of the region, to our allies in Europe, and to our own security here in the United States.

Question. After the withdrawal from Iraq of U.S. forces at the end of 2011, sectarian strife grew stronger as Prime Minister Maliki targeted his Sunni adversaries who, in turn began talking about Maliki's ''power grab.'' President Obama has made it clear that he views the collapse of the Iraqi Security Forces as a failure of Iraqi leaders to build an inclusive government.

♦(a) How hard did the administration work after the withdrawal of U.S. forces to help Maliki maintain an inclusive government?

Answer. Advancing Iraq's democracy is a key component of our relationship under the U.S.-Iraq Strategic Framework Agreement, and we continue to work with Iraqis across the political spectrum and civil society to advance that agenda. We have repeatedly urged the Iraqi Government to uphold its commitments to due process and the rule of law as enshrined in its constitution and to avoid any actions that exacerbate sectarian tensions.

♦(b) How long did this diplomatic effort remain a priority for the administration?

Answer. The need for inclusive government and political reconciliation has been a focus of our conversations with Prime Minister Maliki and other Iraqi leaders since PM Maliki's government was first formed, and we have used high-level meeting, including Prime Minister Maliki's visits to Washington in January 2012 and November 2013, to reinforce that message.

♦(c) Who specifically is the administration working with now in the Sunni community to restore credibility to the central government?

Answer. We believe that the only way to restore credibility to the central government in Iraq is through the formation of an inclusive government, and to this end we have been fully engaged with Iraqi officials, politicians, civil society leaders, and religious leaders from all components of Iraqi society. Following Iraq's successful parliamentary elections on April 30, our priority has been to ensure that the government formation process stays on track, especially in light of the threat that the Islamic State of Iraq and the Levant (ISIL) poses to Iraq. To support this goal, Vice President Biden and former Speaker Nujaifi spoke over the telephone in June about the continued need for political reconciliation and an inclusive government, and Deputy Assistant Secretary McGurk met repeatedly with Iraqi leaders in June and

74

July to ensure that the government formation process followed the constitutionally mandated timeline.

Within the Iraqi Sunni community we continue to engage with national and local Sunni officials and tribal leaders to promote the formation of an inclusive government that would address Sunni grievances. That message has been reinforced, in coordination with international partners, by encouraging Iraq's Sunni neighbors to support Iraqi Sunni participation in the government formation process.

Question. The void created by the withdrawal of American troops at the end of 2011 was supposed to be filled by a robust diplomatic presence at our state-of-the-art Embassy in Baghdad, and two consulates in Basrah and Erbil. In 2012, personnel numbered above 12,000. In 2013, we were at 10,500, and current reports suggest that there are 5,500 personnel there, including contractors, though the State Department has apparently declined to disclose the official numbers of diplomatic personnel in Iraq.

♦(a) What are the official numbers of diplomatic personnel—including contractors—in Iraq for 2012, 2013 and at present?

Answer. In January 2012, at the time of the transition, the number of all personnel (U.S., third country national, and local staff—both direct hire and contractor) under Chief of Mission authority was about 16,000. This decreased to about 10,500 by September 2013 and further to about 5,500 in May 2014. After the relocation of personnel from Baghdad over the past 6 weeks, as of July 24 our on-the-ground staffing for Chief of Mission personnel countrywide is about 4,700, including 740 direct hires and 3,960 contractors. Of these 4,700, about 1,860 are Americans.

♦(b) What effort was made by this diplomatic corps to work with the central government to remain an inclusive body?

Answer. Our mission is fully engaged with Iraqi officials, politicians, and religious and social leaders at all levels and across the political spectrum. U.S. engagement remains focused on supporting the constitutional system and strengthening institutions which transcend the interests of individuals, political parties, or sectarian components of Iraqi society. Despite the dangers, over the past few months our diplomatic staff on the ground in Iraq have been focused on first ensuring that the April elections were timely, transparent, and secure, and now continue to play a crucial role in keeping the process for forming a new, inclusive Iraqi Government on track. I personally spent 7 weeks on the ground during the early stages of the ISIL incursion into Ninewah province and worked with leaders on all sides to ensure swift and inclusive government formation. As a result of our collective efforts, the Iraqi Government remains on track to choose a Prime Minister and continue the constitutionally driven government formation process.

More broadly, the United States continues to play an important role by encouraging direct dialogue between Iraq's leaders and political parties. Our political role in Iraq is as a trusted party that provides advice, facilitates communication within and between the various factions, and urges all sides to work together for constructive change. Under the U.S.-Iraq Strategic Framework Agreement, we cooperate with Iraqis across a broad range of issues, including security and defense, economics/trade, and education/culture.

♦(c) Why did the numbers of personnel in Iraq decline so quickly, particularly after the amount of money that was spent to construct our diplomatic facilities there?

Answer. From January 2012 to January 2014, we made significant strides in reducing Chief of Mission personnel throughout Iraq. We reduced our footprint from 13 sites, including those for Office of Security Cooperation and Foreign Military Sales operations, to 4. We streamlined programs and right-sized our staff. In the summer of 2013, we switched from a DOD-legacy life support contractor to a State-sponsored contractor, significantly reducing the number of contractors countrywide. Although we have significantly reduced overall numbers of personnel, all of our diplomatic facilities remain fully utilized since we have pulled personnel in to operate from these sites as peripheral sites have been closed.

RESPONSES OF ELISSA SLOTKIN TO QUESTIONS
SUBMITTED BY SENATOR JEFF FLAKE

ISIL ADVANCE INTO MOSUL

Question. The administration has blamed Baghdad for not heeding U.S. warnings about ISIL's impending advance into Mosul.

◆ Was it a surprise when ISIL took control over Fallujah earlier this year?
◆ Did the administration warn Baghdad or share intelligence with officials there preceding the ISIL takeover of Fallujah?
◆ How long has ISIL been of concern to the administration?

Answer. We were surprised by the speed at which four Iraqi divisions melted away in some areas, and some areas where they simply did not fight, in contrast to western Iraq where Iraqi Security Forces (ISF) put up a serious fight. Rather than a lack of capability, these actions revealed that some units within the ISF lack either the will or the direction to fight. Understanding these matters better is critical in deciding on any future plans to pursue in Iraq. That is why we have U.S. Forces on the ground right now trying to figure that out. Regarding whether we shared intelligence with Baghdad, I defer to my State colleague. We have long considered ISIL a concern, and we began working with the Government of Iraq in early January to bolster their ability to counter ISIL through increased security cooperation and expedited sales of defense articles.

U.S. GOALS IN IRAQ

Question. The United States has sat back and watched while ISIL took control of Fallujah, Mosul, Tikrit, and moved into Diyala province. The U.S. has sent 300 advisors to Iraq and air strikes remain an option still under review. According to CRS, "U.S. officials express increasing confidence that the IS-led offensive will not be able to capture [Baghdad] outright, although the ISF might yet lose parts of the city."

◆ What are the administration's goals in Iraq?
◆ What does it hope to achieve with the sending of advisors to aid the ISF?
◆ Are we content with letting ISIL maintain control over the territory it's already claimed?

Answer. As the President said on July 19, the administration is focused on maintaining and ensuring the security of the U.S. Embassy and U.S. personnel operating inside of Iraq; increasing the U.S. intelligence picture of the situation in Iraq; and setting up the infrastructure to support the Iraqis through shared intelligence and coordinating planning to counter ISIL. The U.S. Central Command assessment team is working to identify and evaluate viable partners within the Iraqi Security Forces. The assessment team will identify viable partners for the United States to support in their fight against this threat.

The intelligence community has assessed that ISIL currently poses a threat to our regional interests and allies. If left unchecked, ISIL may eventually threaten the homeland. It is not in the interest of the United States to allow ISIL to maintain the territory it seized. A safe haven will allow ISIL to consolidate further and continue to threaten the United States and its allies.

U.S. WITHDRAWAL FROM IRAQ

Question. After the withdrawal from Iraq of U.S. forces at the end of 2011, sectarian strife grew stronger as Prime Minister Maliki targeted his Sunni adversaries who, in turn began talking about Maliki's "power grab." President Obama has made it clear that he views the collapse of the Iraqi Security Forces as a failure of Iraqi leaders to build an inclusive government.

◆ How hard did the administration work after the withdrawal of U.S. forces to help Maliki maintain an inclusive government?
◆ For how long did this diplomatic effort remain a priority for the administration?
◆ Who specifically is the administration working with now in the Sunni community to restore credibility to the central government?

Answer. These are primarily diplomatic matters, and I defer to my State Department colleagues to provide more information.

Question. The void created by the withdrawal of American troops at the end of 2011 was supposed to be filled by a robust diplomatic presence at our state-of-the-art Embassy in Baghdad, and two consulates in Basrah and Erbil. In 2012, personnel numbered above 12,000. In 2013, we were at 10,500, and current reports suggest that there are 5,500 personnel there, including contractors, though the State Department has apparently declined to disclose the official numbers of diplomatic personnel in Iraq.

◆ What are the official numbers of diplomatic personnel—including contractors—in Iraq for 2012, 2013, and at present?
◆ What effort was made by this diplomatic corps to work with the central government to remain an inclusive body?

♦ Why did the numbers of personnel in Iraq decline so quickly, particularly after the amount of money that was spent to construct our diplomatic facilities there?

Answer. These are primarily diplomatic matters, and I defer to my State Department colleagues to provide more information.

RESPONSES OF BRETT MCGURK TO QUESTIONS
SUBMITTED BY SENATOR JOHN BARRASSO

POLITICAL SITUATION

On July 15, the Iraqi Parliament elected a moderate Sunni to the Speaker of Parliament.

In the coming days, we expect the Parliament to elect a President that will replace Talibani.

It appears to me that the security situation in Iraq will not improve until a new Prime Minister is elected.

The Iraq Constitution requires the Parliament to pick a Prime Minister within 75 days from when date of when it convenes.

The last time Parliament met to pick a Prime Minister, it took nearly 10 months.

Question. What timeline are we looking at for a new Prime Minister?

Answer. Iraq's Constitution lays out a brisk set of timeline for the country's government formation process, including selection of a new Prime Minister. Those constitutional were not adhered too closely by Iraqi leaders following Iraq's general elections in 2010. In contrast with 2010 and in part reflecting our robust diplomatic engagement with top leaders across Iraq's political spectrum, Iraq's new Council of Representatives (COR) has been meeting its constitutional timelines—for example, by convening its first session on July 1 and electing new COR Speaker Salim al-Jabouri, a widely respected Sunni leader, on July 16.

On July 24, the same day as this hearing and well within constitutional timelines, the COR elected senior Kurdish political leader Fuad Masum to succeed Jelal Talabani as President of Iraq. Masum's election represents another key milestone in Iraq's Government formation process and an important compromise among Iraq's ethnosectarian political blocs. We fully expect President Masum to execute his constitutional responsibilities by directing the largest bloc in the COR to form a new Cabinet, including a new Prime Minister, for the COR's approval by September 8 in accordance with Iraq's constitutional timelines.

Question. As long as President al-Maliki is in power, what is your assessment of the chances to reconstitute the Iraqi Security Forces (ISF)?

Answer. There continues to be significant opposition to electing Nuri al-Maliki for a third term as Prime Minister, which could complicate efforts to build broad-based political support for the ISF's reconstitution. However, Maliki will remain Iraq's Prime Minister until newly elected President of Iraq Fuad Masum directs the largest bloc in Iraq's Council of Representatives (COR) to nominate a new Prime Minister for the COR's approval, under Iraq's Constitution by September 8, and the COR confirms the nominee. We continue to engage with Iraqi leaders from all ethnoreligious blocs to come together around a candidate for Prime Minister who can unify Iraq against the Islamic State in Iraq and the Levant (ISIL). Until a new Prime Minister is elected, we must and will continue working with Prime Minister Maliki to ensure the ISF's swift reconstitution, which is supported by all major political parties inside and outside Prime Minister Maliki's coalition.

Question. In your assessment, what are the chances of Maliki stepping down?

Answer. Nuri al-Maliki will remain Iraq's Prime Minister until newly elected President of Iraq Fuad Massum directs the largest bloc in Iraq's Council of Representatives (COR) to nominate a new Prime Minister for the COR's approval, by September 8 under Iraq's Constitution, and the COR confirms that nominee. Buoyed by a record 721,000 personal votes in Iraq's historic general elections on April 30, Prime Minister Maliki continues to insist publicly that he will seek another term as Prime Minister. Meanwhile, there appears to be growing sentiment within all of Iraq's societal components that Iraq would be more unified with new leadership—a sentiment Maliki at times seems to acknowledge to some extent.

We continue to engage with top Iraqi political, civic, and religious leaders from all blocs to come together around a candidate for Prime Minister who can unify Iraq against the Islamic State in Iraq and the Levant (ISIL). Until a new Prime Minister is elected, we must and will continue working with Prime Minister Maliki in aiding the Government of Iraq in defending Iraq's territorial integrity against ISIL, which is supported by all major political parties inside and outside Prime Minister Maliki's coalition. If Iraqis' duly elected representatives choose another Prime Minister, the United States will continue its support for Iraq to that same end.

Question. Are we seeing any efforts within Iraq and the Shiite population to pressure the President Maliki to step down?

Answer. There appears to be growing sentiment within all of Iraq's societal components, including Iraq's Shia population, that Iraq would be more unified with new leadership. For example, Grand Ayatollah Ali Husayni al-Sistani, Iraq's most senior Shia cleric, has repeatedly called for the formation of a new Iraqi Government and in a recent sermon admonished Iraqi leaders against sacrificing the country's future for their own political interests—sentiments echoed in a statement from Maliki's Islamic Dawa Party that same day. Despite pressure from many in Iraq's Shia community, Maliki seemingly remains buoyed by his record 721,000 personal votes in Iraq's historic general elections on April 30 and continues to insist publicly that he will seek another term as Prime Minister.

We continue to engage with top Iraqi political, civic, and religious leaders from all blocs, including Iraq's Shia community, to come together around a candidate for Prime Minister who can unify Iraq against the Islamic State in Iraq and the Levant (ISIL). However, that decision must be made by Iraqi lawmakers. Until a new Prime Minister is elected, we must and will continue working with Prime Minister Maliki in aiding the Government of Iraq in defending Iraq's territorial integrity against ISIL.

Question. Should Maliki step down, who are the likely successors to take over?

Answer. When newly elected President of Iraq Fuad Masum directs the largest bloc within Iraq's Council of Representatives (COR) to form a new Cabinet, that bloc will almost certainly be composed of primarily Shia parties, which can be expected to nominate a Shia leader for the COR to confirm as Iraq's Prime Minister. Should current Prime Minister Maliki decline his renomination or the largest COR bloc identifies another candidate, there a number of frequently mentioned alternatives—including several senior leaders within Prime Minister Maliki's State of Law coalition—which performed well in Iraq's historic general elections on April 30.

Regardless of party or ethnoreligious affiliation, we will continue to press all political blocs to support a candidate for Prime Minister who can govern inclusively and thereby unify all Iraqis against the Islamic State in Iraq and the Levant.

AIR STRIKES

Question. For years the Iraqis have been asking for our assistance in providing military aircraft to combat al-Qaeda and ISIS fighters throughout Iraq. This year and reportedly in 2013, the Iraqis have requested our assistance to launch air strikes against ISIS.

Recently, Mr. McGurk stated before House Foreign Affairs Committee that Iraq did not formally request air support until May 2013.

- ◆ Did the Iraqis request air support to combat ISIS forces in 2013?
- ◆ Can you please differentiate between formal and informal requests for air support?
- ◆ What are the current options for airstrikes on ISIS forces?
- ◆ How do we plan on differentiating Iraq Security Forces, Kurdish Security Forces, and Iran Security Forces from the ISIS?
- ◆ With the United States, Iraq, Iran, and Russia currently operating in Iraq airspace, how are we currently deconflicting our Intelligence, Surveillance and Reconnaissance (ISR) operations?

Answer. The Iraqis formally requested air support in May 2014. Prior to the formal requests, Iraqi officials made informal inquiries regarding capabilities, to include airstrikes, but these conversations never escalated to the requisite level of coordination necessary within the GOI. With the formal request, airspace permissions, coordination and GOI political support, the President authorized prompt action, to include combat operations by U.S. aircraft, and CENTCOM surged ISR flights over the region.

Since that time, President Obama has made it clear that he will take action, including military action, at a time and place of our choosing, if and when it is necessary to defend our national security interests. We are continuing to improve our intelligence picture of the situation on the ground so we can assess potential options. The two Joint Operations Centers in Baghdad and Erbil are augmenting this effort as they enhance information-sharing relationships. Airstrikes without the

78

necessary intelligence would be irresponsible and would not make any operational impact on the ground.

We would defer to DOD for specifics for airspace deconfliction.

———

RESPONSES OF ELISSA SLOTKIN TO QUESTIONS
SUBMITTED BY SENATOR JOHN BARRASSO

ASSESSMENT OF IRAQ SECURITY FORCES

Question. How long do we assess that it will take to recruit, train, and equip new forces to reconstitute the four divisions that have been reduced?

Answer. The U.S. Central Command assessment team is still in the process of identifying and assessing potential partners within the Iraqi Security Forces. We continue to update the initial assessment that the team provided the week of July 14, and developing options, but it is too early in that process to provide more detail.

Question. Please outline President al Maliki's actions that led to the crumbling of the Iraqi Security Forces under his leadership?

Answer. The Iraq Security Forces' (ISF) losses are the result of Iraqi political divisions and leadership challenges. As the President said on June 19, it's not any secret that there are deep divisions between Sunni, Shia, and Kurdish leaders, and those divisions made it difficult for the Government of Iraq (GOI) to command the ISF directly in its efforts to combat ISIL. We are focused now on encouraging the GOI to move forward with the government formation process, and in ensuring that competent military leaders are put in place in key posts.

Question. Does the Pentagon have a timeline on when it will make its recommendations to the President on how to proceed in Iraq?

Answer. The Secretary of Defense has provided his views regularly to the President on how to proceed in Iraq. The Chairman of the Joint Chiefs of Staff has provided his best military advice. This advice informs the options available to the President on future action in Iraq. The National Security Council will make recommendations to the President.

AIR STRIKES

Question. For years the Iraqis have been asking for our assistance in providing military aircraft to combat al-Qaeda and ISIS fighters throughout Iraq. This year and reportedly in 2013, the Iraqis have requested our assistance to launch air strikes against ISIS. Recently, Mr. McGurk stated before House Foreign Affairs Committee that Iraq did not formally request air support until May 2013.

♦ Did the Iraqis request air support to combat ISIS forces in 2013?
♦ Can you please differentiate between formal and informal requests for air support?
♦ What are the current options for airstrikes on ISIS forces?
♦ How do we plan on differentiating Iraq Security Forces, Kurdish Security Forces, and Iran Security Forces from the ISIS?
♦ With the U.S., Iraq, Iran, and Russia currently operating in Iraq airspace, how we are currently de-conflicting our Intelligence, Surveillance, and Reconnaissance (ISR) operations?

Answer. The Iraqis did not request air support in 2013. U.S. Government representatives had regular conversations with GOI counterparts on how best to counter ISIL. As the security situation in Iraq deteriorated, the Government of Iraq (GOI) requested expedited defense equipment and increased training, which the United States provided.

But the GOI did not formally request air strikes until recently. As directed by the President, we are looking at the full range of options on future action in Iraq, to include air support.

We are in continuous contact with the Iraqis to ensure close coordination on our activities. But to be clear, we are not coordinating military activity with Iran or Russia.